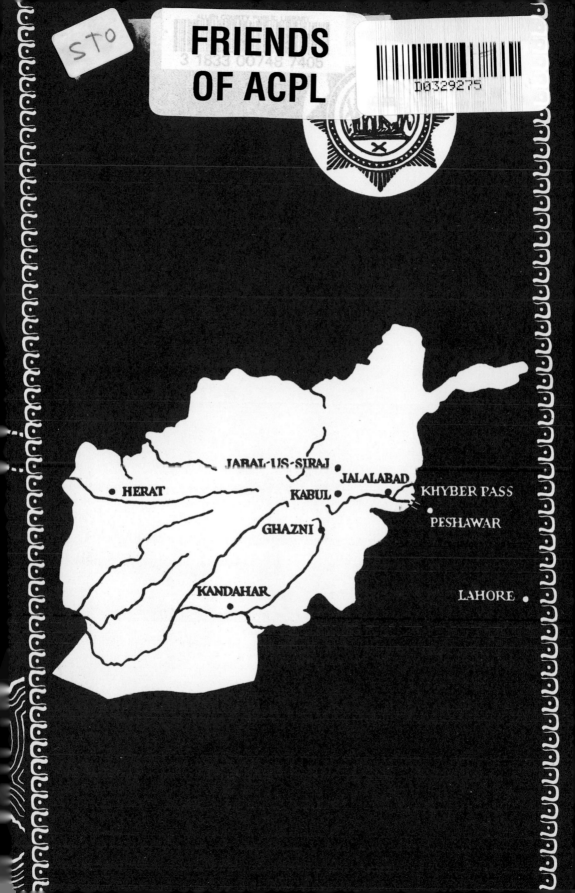

HERAT

JABAL-US-SIRAJ

KABUL

JALALABAD

KHYBER PASS

PESHAWAR

GHAZNI

KANDAHAR

LAHORE

Other books by Christine Weston

THE DARK WOOD (*a novel*)
THE WISE CHILDREN (*a novel*)
THE WORLD IS A BRIDGE (*a novel*)
INDIGO (*a novel*)
THE DEVIL'S FOOT (*a novel*)
BE THOU THE BRIDE (*a novel*)
THERE AND THEN (*stories*)
BHIMSA THE DANCING BEAR (*a children's book*)

WORLD BACKGROUND BOOKS

AFGHANISTAN by Christine Weston
CEYLON by Christine Weston
THE NEW AFRICA by Ellen and Attilio Gatti
MEDITERRANEAN SPOTLIGHTS by Attilio Gatti
HERE IS INDIA (*Revised Edition*) by Jean Kennedy
WITHIN THE CIRCLE by Evelyn Stefansson
HERE IS THE FAR NORTH by Evelyn Stefansson
HERE IS ALASKA (*Revised Edition*) by Evelyn Stefansson

Afghanistan

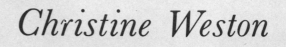
Christine Weston

A WORLD BACKGROUND BOOK

AFGHANISTAN

Illustrated with photographs and a map

CHARLES SCRIBNER'S SONS

NEW YORK

This book published simultaneously in the United States of America and in Canada—Copyright under the Berne Convention

A-10.62[UJ]

Acknowledgments

The lines from "Arithmetic on the Frontier," "The Young British Soldier," "The Ballad of East and West," from *Departmental Ditties and Ballads and Barrack-Room Ballads* by Rudyard Kipling are reprinted by permission of Mrs. George Bambridge, Doubleday and Company, Inc., and the Macmillan Company of Canada Ltd.

The endpapers are reproduced by permission of the University of Minnesota Press, Minneapolis from *An American Engineer in Afghanistan* by Marjorie Jewett Bell. Copyright 1948 by the University of Minnesota.

Printed in the United States of America

Library of Congress Catalog Card Number 62-15498

Acknowledgments

Grateful acknowledgment is made for permission to use the following:

Photographs on pages 4, 6, 18, 20, 27, 28, 29, 44, 49, 50, 69, 76, 78, 80, 86, 89, 90, 96, 99, 101, 102, 104, 109, 112, 115, 121, 122, 124–125, 126, 150–151, 153 by Christine Weston

Photographs on pages 2–3, 16–17, 24, 47, 52–53, 73, 110, 116, 117, 130–131 by Rolando Schinasi from Monkmeyer Press Photo Service

Photographs on pages 9, 22–23, 32, 36–37, 42, 56, 94–95, 106, 138, 141, 143, 144, 146 by James Cudney from Agency for International Development

Photographs on title page and pages 13, 61, 84, 97, 136–137 by John di Cara

Photographs on pages 35, 66, 81, 149 by Stephanie Dinkins

Photograph on pages 40–41 from the Morrison-Knudsen Company, Inc.

Map on pages 62–63 by Rafael Palacios

For Radhi Uttam Singh

Contents

List of Illustrations

Afghanistan

CHAPTER ONE
En Route

It was on a humid morning in April that I boarded an Afghan Airways plane (that old dependable, a DC-3) at Palam airport in New Delhi, bound for Kabul, the capital of Afghanistan, via Amritsar in India's Punjab province. I had had to wait until April to make the flight, because Kabul stands at 6,900 feet and is snowbound for six months of the year.

There were six people aboard the plane: the pilot and co-pilot—both Indians, a young Indian steward, an Indian businessman, and two Americans—myself and a professor from Columbia University, the latter working with the Agency of International Development assistance program at the University of Kabul.

The Hindu Kush mountains in winter

All but four seats in the cabin had been removed to make room for bales and boxes of merchandise, and as the plane taxied down the airstrip, I flattered myself that we were in the great tradition of travelers, people with a single-minded purpose: one of us a teacher, one a writer, the other a merchant, modest enough in our aspirations, yet moved by something better than a mere impulse to shop and sight-see.

We readied for the take-off, and names echoed in my ears, a sort of accompaniment to the rhythm of the propellers: Alexander the Great, Hiuen Tsang, Marco Polo, Zoroaster, Omar Khayyam, not to mention a lesser galaxy of adventurers, among them relatives of mine, who had come this way as soldiers and administrators in more recent times. On foot or on horseback, all had followed the routes of the great trade caravans, out of India toward the passes of Afghanistan and Persia, or in reverse, down into India. Time then had an especial urgency in its relation to climate and terrain: a pass must be traversed, a river crossed, before rain and darkness added to the peril.

Those early travelers were probably conscious of their world in a peculiarly intimate fashion. They felt it underfoot and through the flimsy walls of tent and caravanserai, and perhaps because of this contact they understood their world better than we understand ours. The old soldiers and travelers were men of scholarship and experience far in advance of their times. We have progressed beyond the bow and arrow, harquebus and coat of mail, beyond mud fort and naked sword, yet we still turn to the chronicles of those first-comers for information pertinent today. Walking beside a wheatfield north of Kabul, I was to hear wild partridges calling on the slopes, and to remember Marco Polo's description of this sound written eight centuries

A present-day caravanserai in northern Afghanistan

before—"Shir dharam ke shakrak!"—which, roughly translated from the Persian, means "I have milk and sugar!"

Now we were airborne and circling the outskirts of New Delhi, and I had a glimpse, lovely in the morning haze, of the square-cut tombs of the Lodi kings, Afghans who conquered Delhi in the fifteenth century, and of whom one of their poets has written:

> For six or seven generations theirs was the Kingdom,
> And all the world wondered at them!

Then New Delhi was behind us, and we were flying over the yellow-white plains of Uttar Pradesh, towns and villages embedded like pebbles in its vastness, the Jamuna River coiling southward, and a deepening hint of green to the north, the Punjab, land of Five Rivers, a fertile prize over which armies and traders and priests and politicians have struggled through the ages. I was flying over country that had known the tread of Alexander the Great, of Baber and Genghis Khan, of the Emperor Asoka, of Akbar and Jahangir, of the viceroys and captains of the British raj and—in my own time—of Mahatma Gandhi's quiet, sandaled feet.

Although I have had my fair share of traveling, I had never been in Afghanistan. Now, perversely, I found myself recalling a conversation I had had with a Swiss doctor recently returned from Kabul. Learning that I planned to visit Afghanistan, he had inquired with an air of concern, "You are going alone?"

"Why not?" I asked.

"Well, it is still a primitive country, and there are practically no facilities for travelers. And furthermore, Afghans don't approve of women going unveiled. I hope you are prepared for . . . well, all kinds of discomfort. Perhaps also for a certain amount of risk."

There is a curious obstinacy in some of us which makes

it impossible for us to renege on our intention no matter what the obstacles or even the risks. I had heard a good deal about both in regard to my projected trip, yet here I was, ten thousand feet in the air, headed for one of the lesser known and least predictable places left in the modern world.

At this point in my reflections—we were about half an hour out of Amritsar—the plane gave a violent jolt and began to shake with a sound and sensation of being torn apart. I met the frozen gaze of the Indian businessman. Then our little steward was on his feet in the aisle, supporting himself by holding the back of my seat, and in a calm voice telling us to fasten our seat belts. The tearing, wrenching noises stopped, the plane steadied, and we were flying at what seemed to be a normal speed, though at a lower altitude. I saw the port propeller standing still, and realized that we were going to try to make Amritsar airport on one engine.

Our steward returned to his seat and I heard him whistling "Colonel Bogey" as we circled for a landing. Far below, I could see the airport and two small bright-red objects scurrying across the tarmac—an ambulance and a fire engine.

Down we floated, slowly, slowly, and as we banked the port wing seemed to point vertically towards the earth. Houses, trees, channels of water rose towards us as if seen through a magnifying glass, and I heard myself whistling "Colonel Bogey" rather tunelessly, through my teeth.

The wheels touched ground and we raced up the strip and came to a smooth stop, and as the four of us—the American professor, the two Indians and myself—rose from our seats, we stared at each other with foolish smiles of mutual congratulation amounting, almost, to affection.

We were told that damage to the plane was such that we would have to spend the night in Amritsar and resume our journey by an Air India plane next day. Afghan Airways

← Street scene in Kabul

provided accommodations for us at a small hostel run by a charming Parsi lady, who made us comfortable, fed us nobly on South Indian curry, and regaled us with stories of disaster and near-disaster that had brought strangers from all parts of the globe to her door.

That evening her daughters played the piano for us and sang English songs which dated to the 1920's and my own girlhood in India. The evening was warm enough to sit outdoors, and after dinner we mounted to the flat roof of the house where, amid the rising fragrance from the garden, the eldest lovely daughter picked amateurishly at a ukelele; the youngest, attired in the typical Punjabi dress of voluminous trousers and loose white shirt with bells tied to her ankles, went through the motions of an Indian dance, artlessly absorbed in what she was doing, while the rest of the family eyed us anxiously for our reactions.

During a pause in the entertainment, the mother turned to me and asked, "You have friends in Kabul?"

I replied that I had neither friends nor acquaintances there. She looked horrified. "You are going to that wild place— *alone?*"

This was an echo of my Swiss friend in New Delhi, and my reply to my hostess was also an echo. "Why not?"

"It is not safe. You do not speak their language. You have no friends there, and there is no proper place for travelers to stay. The Afghans do not care for strangers, white strangers especially, and they frown on unveiled women."

I asked whether she had been in Afghanistan and she replied with energy that she certainly had not, nor had she any intention of going. She had, however, heard stories, and proceeded to tell me some, all of them bloodcurdling and calculated to put a damper on the hardiest spirit.

"You had better stay here with us," she ended, firmly.

The donkey and shanks' mare are popular modes of travel in Afghanistan

"There is plenty you could write about in Amritsar. It would be much safer for you, and you could tell us all about America."

We were interrupted by the arrival of an airport official who informed us jovially that all was well, and that the next morning at ten o'clock sharp we were to proceed to Kabul by Air India Flight 21. His smile was effulgent. "May God be with you then," he said, "as He was today!"

The morning dawned clear and beautiful, and by ten-thirty we were airborne—the professor from Columbia, the Indian businessman, myself, and two other passengers whom we had taken on at Amritsar: an austere-looking Russian carrying a brief case, and a man who appeared to be his bodyguard, a stalwart Pathan in baggy breeches and huge black turban. A curved four-foot knife hung from the Pathan's shoulder by a leather strap.

Amritsar and its golden temples dissolved beneath us, and in a little while I saw, lifting their peaks above the pale blue wash of light, the mountain ranges of Afghanistan.

CHAPTER TWO

Arrival

The Sulaiman range lay bleached and grim to west and south. To the north and northeast, magnificent and frightening, stretched the mountains of the Hindu Kush, or Hindu Killers, a name derived from the fact that in ancient times slaves brought from India perished here like flies from exposure and cold.

The encyclopedia tells us that Afghanistan comprises an area of about 245,000 square miles, roughly the size of Texas. It is bordered to the north by Russian Turkistan, to the west by Iran, to the northeast by Sinkiang, and to the east and south by Pakistan. The population is said to be approximately twelve million and the country is entirely landlocked.

The face of Afghanistan seen from the air or on maps resembles nothing so much as the cratered surface of the moon, or a relief drawing of the ocean floor with its waters drained away to reveal a desolate landscape of peaks and valleys and sinister fissures which snake away towards the frontiers of Russia, China, and Iran and down to the plains of India and Pakistan.

11

These fissures, crisscrossing the country from one end to the other, are the mountain passes. They are among the most distinctive features of Afghanistan and serve it for transportation and trade. The routes remain as they were through centuries: the Margalla Pass, the Malakand, Bolan, Kurram, Qipchak, Shibar, and Khyber. They are names famous in history, avenues down which successive waves of invasion have poured on their way to the conquest of India, and along which other invasions, headed in the opposite direction, have surged in one attempt after another to subdue a people who, so far, have resisted every effort of foreign domination.

Afghanistan as yet has no railroad system, and her rivers are for the most part unsuited to anything except the most primitive forms of navigation. There are no more than two or three airfields, active only during the summer months. While the development of air travel, both for civil and military purposes, has probably lessened the importance of the mountain passes, they remain indispensable to the economy of the country as a whole. Only a handful of the people can afford to travel by air; the chief means of locomotion for the common man are still the bus, the camel, the donkey, or his own two feet. The great majority of the people use the passes just as their forefathers did, though today we can see almost as many buses as camels. What once were stony tracks or temporary rivers of mud are now modern highways with dual lanes, one for pack animals, the other for automobiles.

The passes of Afghanistan serve the country in much the same fashion as the great river systems of Europe and other parts of the Middle and Far East serve those countries. The Khyber is probably the most important of the passes between Pakistan and Afghanistan, with an area of about 962 miles and a population of around 216,662.

It has its beginnings roughly twenty-five miles north of the great city of Peshawar in Pakistan. Peshawar has been identified by some writers as the original Paskpuros of Herodotus, a prize towards which Afghan conquerors from the north, and Hindu, Sikh, and British from the south, have always cast a longing eye. Peshawar was visited by Alexander the Great. It was for many years the winter capital of the Mogul emperors and scene of some of the bloodiest battles between Sikhs and Afghans in later times. It is now one of the most important cities in western Pakistan.

The Khyber is a narrow defile which runs between high cliffs of shale and limestone. Not even the Brenner Pass between Italy and Austria has quite the strategic importance of the Khyber or anything like its checkered history. While there is no proof

This sign indicates two-lane traffic through the Khyber Pass

that Alexander the Great used the Khyber for his descent into India in 327 B.C., it is believed by some writers that his general, Hephaestion, came through the Khyber into the Peshawar plain, and this was certainly the route followed by two later conquerors of India—Mahmud of Ghazni, and the great Baber.

Today, ancient Sikh and Afghan fortresses and the more recent picket posts and pillboxes built by the British to stand off Afghan and Pathan raiders, dot the entire area. They remind one that what is now for the most part a modern highway was as recently as twenty years ago a military road of prime importance to the power which controlled it, and to others who might have an eye to controlling it themselves.

The Khyber gets its name from the Khyber Hills through which it runs, beginning about three miles beyond Fort Jamrud and continuing for about thirty miles to the barren plain of Loi Dakka, which stretches to the banks of the Kabul River near the village of Lalpura. Throughout its length the Khyber threads the country of the great Pathan tribes—the Kuki Khel (khel means tribe), the Sipali, Shinwari, the Zakka Khel, names which carry the ring of the Scottish clans to whom they have been likened.

In the sixteenth century the Mogul Emperor Akbar's chief engineer, Quasim Khan, built the first road through the Khyber, making it passable for wheeled traffic. Before that the route was scarcely practicable for horses and camels.

Some travelers have described the Khyber Pass as grim and forbidding, but there are others for whom it holds a peculiar fascination. Just as a great river excites one's imagination by the thought of its passage through miles of unknown country, past strange peoples and stranger scenery, and by the knowledge that it has existed, restless and ever flowing, not only through physical space but through time, so these rather fearful clefts in the barren hills of Afghanistan bemuse anyone not easily intimidated by the unfamiliar, and by a sense of time standing, so to speak, still and watchful in its tracks.

Years have seen great changes in the Khyber country, but the shale and limestone formations which excited the curiosity of Hephaestion remain what they have always been, and the contours of the stony hills against the sky have not changed since Akbar's day and before. Not only the great conquerors but their followers, the nameless phalanx of the Greeks, not only Mahmud of Ghazni and the poet-soldier Baber, nor the captains and the kings of a later time—not these only, but whole processions of humbler men whose origins are lost in mystery and whose end is not in sight, have gazed where we gaze now, on the very stone, the very curve of the river, the very spot where the sky seems to lean its elbow on the hard brown shoulder of the hill beyond Jamrud.

Today we can fly from the modern airports of Moscow or Teheran, New Delhi or Peshawar, directly to the ticklish landing on the narrow airstrip at Kabul, capital of Afghanistan—Kabul, city of sinister memories, of which a traveler safely returned to his own country once wrote:

> There have I traveled, too—but I
> Saw naught, said naught, and—did not die!

As our plane banked over the airstrip, the bare brown hills which encircle the city tilted upward to reveal eroded shapes of ancient battlements with crenelated walls and crumbling bastions, and the squat brown bulk of the Bala Hisar, where a British envoy to Afghanistan and his entire escort of soldiers were massacred on the outbreak of the Second Afghan War in 1878. The new Bala Hisar is now an arsenal for the Afghan army and forbidden territory to outsiders.

Kabul means sheepfold. I asked myself, could this savage, historic city ever have been anything so mild and unassuming

The route from Peshawar to Kabul crosses the Tanghi Gharu gorge →

In the valley of the Bamian

as a stockaded village harboring shepherds and their flocks? Yet so it had started centuries ago, before becoming the turbulent capital and jumping-off place for Turkish, Mongol, Persian, and Afghan adventurers bent on conquest of the rich Indian plains to the south.

I thought of Baber, first of the great Mogul emperors, conqueror of Afghanistan and India, lying buried under enormous plane trees in the lovely garden overlooking the city, and of the conquerors and rulers who came after him: Akbar and Jahangir, Ahmad Shah, the brilliant, cruel, and humorous Abd-er-Rahman Khan, and of Amir Amanullah, king of Afghanistan, whose tragi-comic passion for reform along modern lines ended in his ignominious exile in 1929. Now these names began to assume a queer intimacy for me, and I felt that indescribable thrill which affects one in a setting where the present seems to merge visibly with the past.

We touched down and skimmed along the tarmac in the shadow of bare brown hills, and I saw a group of old men with long white beards, looking as if they had stepped out of the Old Testament, and a small boy in a big turban, flying a paper kite. Then, as I made my way towards the terminal buildings, an American woman, a total stranger, hailed me in the familiar and unexpected accents of home. "If you have no place to stay, come along with us!"

Accommodations in Kabul were few and far between, and the American contingent with the United Nations and related agencies made it their business to see that homeless migrants like myself had some place to lay their heads.

We drove away from the airport, and Kabul, its blue-domed mosques, its wide bazaars, and its bridges spanning the Kabul River, opened before me. There was something positive and exhilarating in the quality of the air, mountain air tasting and smelling of great heights, and a feeling of nearness to a sky of the purest blue I had ever seen.

My companions told me that the road we took had been paved by Russian engineers, who had also paved the main streets of the city as a gesture of goodwill towards Afghanistan.

At this point a car passed us, going in the same direction, and I recognized one of the passengers as the austere Russian with the brief case, my fellow passenger from Amritsar, and, in the back seat, resplendent in his black turban and carrying his four-foot sword, the Pathan bodyguard—or could he have been the watchdog?

History teaches us that every landlocked nation faces immemorial problems of sovereignty, language, and communication.

Afghan boy
carrying water jug,
outside Kabul

These problems have not lessened with the new alignment of frontiers between Afghanistan and her neighbors. If anything, they have increased.

The Russians are said to have spent $20,000,000 to $100,-000,000 in helping to equip and train the Afghan Army and Air Force, besides paving the streets of the capital, providing most of the buses and automobiles, the gasoline and oil. They have also built a wheat silo, a flour mill, and a machine-tool factory.

The United States has contributed around $180,000,000 mostly in reclamation projects in the south, the remainder in agriculture, transportation, public administration, and education. There seems to be a neck-and-neck race to see who can do the most for the Afghans, a somewhat different form of invasion compared to those in the not too distant past, when the foreigner was apt to appear bearing not peace but a sword.

CHAPTER THREE
Kabul, the Capital

An Afghan friend of mine made the observation that in
Afghanistan all roads start from Kabul and end in Kabul, and
this seems to be as good a description of the capital's importance
as any I can think of. Whether we arrive at Kabul by air, or via
the somber throat of the Khyber Pass, we soon realize that we
are at the heart of the nation, its nerve center, from which the
entire country is administered and controlled. Kabul is the
residence of the king, the seat of government, headquarters for

22

View of Kabul

the army, militia, and police, site of all the foreign embassies and consulates, and operational center for the United Nations effort in Afghanistan.

"That wild place!" as my Parsi hostess had described it, turned out to be a curious mixture of things familiar and things utterly strange. Automobiles, buses, and trucks; electricity, radios, the sight of an occasional American or European face—these are familiar. But aside from the broad main streets and sprawling bazaars, the rest is mystery. High walls and barred doors keep one at arm's length from the intimate life of the people, and although Kabul has an estimated population of about 200,000, there is none of the sense of crowding one feels in other Eastern cities of comparable size. Slowly, we realize that this to a great extent is due to the relative absence of women. They are there, behind the high mud walls, behind the barred windows and closed gates, or scurrying along the streets shrouded in their chadris, zombie-like garments of drab colors which cover the wearers from head to toe and which present-day Afghan society compels women to wear in public.

And there is the strangeness of language, of which there are two: Persian and Pashto, both spoken by few of the Europeans and Americans in the country, just as a handful of upper-class, educated Afghans can speak English. I was lucky to find an English-speaking Afghan, a charming and intelli-

A secondhand clothes vendor arranges his wares in Kabul

gent young man who acted as interpreter and guide to me, and without whose genial and understanding cooperation I would have had a hard time.

What sinks most forcibly into one's consciousness is a sense of Kabul's difference from other Eastern capitals, Colombo for instance, or New Delhi, or Cairo. For all that these are Eastern in essence, they nevertheless include an age-old cosmopolitanism, architecturally and in the dress and language of their citizens. But this is not true of Kabul.

Despite the presence of electric power and radios, a movie theater, solid government buildings, palaces and schools, an efficient telephone system which links the capital with the rest of the country—despite all these, and the introduction here and there of Westernized dress on some of the men, the city gives an impression of having remained unchanged for the past one hundred years.

The old part of the city is still unpaved, and it is here one finds the bazaars, with their little cubbyhole shops where merchants sit behind their wares, selling anything from carpets to pistachio nuts, both products of the country. One sees tea-shops, silversmiths, workers in gold and lapis lazuli (the latter also a product of the country), and vegetable stalls piled high with fresh tomatoes, cauliflowers, and beautiful bright-green heads of lettuce which the children eat with as much relish as American children eat ice cream.

Some of the shops sell karakul skins and karakul caps for men. These caps come in three degrees of fineness: the best and most expensive is a sort of honey-brown color, the next a glossy black, and the cheapest and most commonly worn is plain gray. Karakul, the pelt of baby karakul or broad-tailed sheep which are raised in great flocks in northern Afghanistan, forms one of the country's basic exports since it is much in demand in Pakistan and throughout the Middle East.

Trains of camels stand or crouch on the ground at intervals along the bazaars. Gardis, two-wheeled carriages drawn by gaily bedizened horses, clatter to and fro, and boys in the traditional baggy trousers, loose flowing shirts, and black turbans, roll iron hoops with fiendish skill in and out among the crowd. One noticeable detail about these boys, who range in age from about seven to ten, is that I hardly recall seeing one who did not carry a slingshot dangling from his wrist. This may account for the dearth of bird life near the settled communities, for the boys learn to be deadly shots. I saw one Nimrod of about ten bring down a pigeon as cleanly as if he had killed it with a rifle.

The buildings in the city are mostly of mud and unbaked brick, with some stucco and paint. Touches of elegance and urbanity merge with areas that seem to be crumbling with age and decay. In Afghanistan the visitor must obtain official permission to take photographs, and it is forbidden to take pictures of military installations, veiled women, and the shabby sections of town. This is a poor country, economically, but Afghans are extremely proud, and the government does not care to have foreigners publicize poverty and backwardness in its native land.

Strolling through the streets of Kabul, I came on a scene which struck me as quite beautiful. It was in a fairly remote quarter, where part of an old building seemed to have fallen away, revealing a pattern of delicately painted walls and shadows. Against this background a group of men were spreading brilliant carpets to air in the sun. I started to take the picture, when from nowhere a policeman appeared and politely but firmly motioned me to desist. He made no objection, however, when, a few minutes later, I took a snapshot of a splendid-looking tribesman with a hooded falcon perched on his wrist, riding a lively horse, for all the world like a figure out of the Arabian Nights.

On another occasion I was about to take a picture of half a dozen little shops clustered together, all of which seemed to specialize in aluminum ware. There were carefully arranged stacks of aluminum dishes, kettles, and pans, and, hanging from the rafters, festoons of knives and forks and spoons. Behind these wares sat the merchants, dignified men wearing turbans and purple, green, or chocolate-colored shirts and shawls. The light was perfect, making the metal glow like moonlight, and bringing out the rich contrasts in the men's clothing. What I did not notice at once was a young soldier standing beside one of the shops. He was dressed in the World War I type of German uniform, complete with peaked cap and jack-boots, and as I got into position to

Afghan boy
readies his slingshot

An Afghan soldier, outside a teahouse in Kabul

take the picture, he approached and shook his finger reprovingly before the lens. When I protested, asking him in English why I should not take a picture of the shops, he pointed gravely at himself and said, in English, "Military installation!"

He apparently thought that I was taking a picture of him, and since my Persian was no better than his English, I realized that there was no use trying to convince him that it was the merchandise, not the Afghan Army, which interested me.

There are many such taboos in connection with taking photographs in Afghanistan. One is not supposed, for instance, to take pictures of veiled women, and the mullahs, members of the theocratic order, often object to being photographed.

However, I found that the average citizen, men particularly, and children, rather enjoyed the attention, and would often pose for me, sometimes rather overdoing it and spoiling the picture.

One of the refreshing aspects of life in Kabul, and this seems to be true of the country as a whole, is the almost total absence of that problem of the East—the itinerant beggar. The Afghans are a Moslem people, and Moslem teaching enjoins giving alms, particularly to the halt, the lame, and the blind; and though I saw several instances of this, it was always done un-

A young Afghan
girl in Kabul

obtrusively and with dignity by giver and taker alike. Nowhere in the country is one subjected to the nuisance and heartache of the whining, clutching hordes that beset the traveler in other parts of the world. Merchants and traders love to bargain. They regard it as a form of sport in which you are expected to play your part, but they will never push their wares at you, and cheating is extremely rare.

Perhaps nowhere in the world, within such a small compass, does the visitor find such a mixture of races—Mongol, Persian, Turkish, Greek—or such distinction of feature and coloring. Unlike the inhabitants of other parts of the Eastern hemisphere, Afghan complexions tan with sun, and I saw many rosy-faced, sunburned children who might have stepped out from Sussex or Maine.

CHAPTER FOUR

The Country

Afghanistan is an independent kingdom situated in south-central Asia at the western end of the Himalayan range, between 29° and 39° North latitude, and 61° and 72° East longitude. It is considered part of the Middle Eastern system of nations, a sort of rib, or perhaps bastion would be a better word, setting that system off from the countries of the true East, such as Pakistan, India, Burma and Ceylon.

The original name of Afghanistan was Aryana, or the land of the Aryans, a race which, according to some Afghan scholars, first appeared in ancient Bactria, in northern Afghanistan. Other Afghan scholars claim descent for their people from King Saul, maintaining that Saul had a grandson named Afghana, who became the father of the Afghan race. This race, through him, is identified with the ten lost tribes of Israel who sought sanctuary in Aryana in Biblical times.

Even today there are Afghans who debate the question and support their views by citing, among other things, certain similarities of nomenclature: the Moslem Yusef, for instance, corresponding with Joseph, Ibrahim with Abraham, Daud

31

with David, and so on. Some Afghans take particular pride in tracing their ancestry to Alexander the Great, linking the Greek's name with the Moslem Iskander, or Sikander. Kandahar, the great Afghan city in the southwest, was at one time Alexander's headquarters, and is named for him. The debate will probably continue indefinitely for lack of proof one way or another, for the truth is, no one can really be sure who the original Afghans were or whence they came.

They are first mentioned by name—Avagana—by an Indian astronomer, Vahara Mihira, in the early sixth century. Later on the Chinese traveler, Hiuen-Tsang, speaks of a tribe called A-p'-o'kien, living in the Sulaiman Mountains, but the earliest Moslem mention of them is in the Huded-al-'Alam, 982 A.D.

In Afghanistan the sense of antiquity seems to have become arrested, so that in the midst of modern technological developments one can never wholly forget the exciting events of history that have occurred here—a memory as thrilling, perhaps, to newcomers as to the illiterate citizen whose knowledge of history, acquired and defined by word of mouth from father to son, is too often confined to his native village and his tribe.

Standing at the crossroads of Asia, Afghanistan has had a great strategic importance throughout its history. Besides containing the vital trade routes from east to west and from north to south, it has been the chief avenue for alien powers from east and west and for Turks and Mongols from the north. In more recent times it tempted the ambitions of two great empires, British and Russian, while in our day it has become a stage for the rival influences of the United States and the Soviet Union.

There was a time when Afghanistan could boast of being the center of vital Asian civilizations, where art and trade flourished in such great cities as Bactria, "The City of Flags," whose banners and turrets were visible from the shores of the Oxus River and the borders of what is now Russian Turkistan,

← The beautiful lakes of Band-i-Amir in northern Afghanistan

twelve miles to the north. Bactria, now known as Balkh, was the birthplace of Zoroaster, also called Zarathustra, a Persian of whom the Parsis of India are the modern followers. And it was in Bactria that Alexander the Great is said to have met and married the lovely Roxana.

I have stood on the ruins of what is left of Bactria, and have looked down on a dusty little market place surrounded by orchards, and watched shaggy Bactrian camels lurch past in the dust, followed by a procession of new Russian trucks on their way to some construction project nearby, and I thought I felt the breath of history blow up from the rubble at my feet, to remind me of the poet who came this way centuries ago, a tentmaker from Khurasan named Omar Khayyam, who wrote:

> When you and I behind the Veil are past,
> Oh, but the long, long while the World shall last,
> Which of our Coming and Departure heeds
> As the Sea's self should heed a pebble-cast.

This impressive country rises in the north to the steppes of the Oxus, known to Afghans as Amu Darya. It is a scene of everlasting snow piercing the purest and bluest of skies, and it follows the range of the Hindu Kush from the Pamirs to the Iranian border, and south to the desert of the Dasht-i-Margo.

South of the principal massif lie the small spurs and valleys of the Taimani country and the Hazarajat, and the watershed of the Helmand River and the Hari Rud. Another spur of the mountain range runs from the Kabul River at the Khyber Pass to Ghazni in the southeast, and this spur is known as the Safed Koh, roughly translated as the White Cone. Between this range and the plateaus of Baluchistan in Pakistan lies the Sulaiman range, after which comes the desert of Registan and the Khwaja Amran mountains. The mountainous areas of Afghanistan vary from a few thousand feet to the marvelous

Ruins of Khaja Mohammed Parsa mosque in Balkh

peak of the highest mountain in the land, Tirich Mir, 25,263 feet above sea level.

It is a country of extremes in almost every sense of the word—a country of high-lying barren plateaus and stretches of desert, of narrow, winding valleys, green with crops and orchards, of wide, dusty plains that remind one of parts of the American Northwest. On the higher levels one finds forests of deodar (the Asian cedar), pine, larch, and on the lower reaches poplars are cultivated extensively to provide shade, protection against erosion, and timber for building. I watched men and boys lovingly at work planting pencil-thin saplings along the water courses and on the edges of fields and highways. They reminded me of an intricate, industrious society of ants, which seems never to pause in the business of building, conserving, and restoring against the relentless pressures of nature and fate.

Afghanistan has a low average rainfall and is largely de-

A section of the Badam-Bagh land and water conservation

pendent for its water supply on the melting snow which, in spring, helps irrigate the regions below 4,000 feet. In many parts of the country irrigation is provided by wells operating on the ancient system of the Persian water-wheel, or by the karez, an ingenious method of channeling water underground from permanent water tables in the foothills.

The climate varies from region to region. North, northeast, and in the mountainous center it resembles that of Switzerland, but is subject to extremes of cold on desert and plain. At Ghazni, with an elevation of 7,280 feet, snow may remain on the ground for several months and the temperature drop to 15° below zero. Kabul, at 6,900 feet, has severe winters; Jalalabad at 1,000 feet is semi-tropical; and Kandahar at 3,500 feet is generally fair and mild.

There are two distinct seasons, the dry and the wet: dry between May and September, rainy between October and April.

domonstration area, north of Kabul

In winter the northern areas are snowbound, highways impass-
able or almost so, and air traffic comes to a stop. Unlike India
and Ceylon, Afghanistan has no monsoon season, and summer
rains are infrequent. The average rainfall for the whole country is no more than twelve inches, though temperatures have a
seasonal and daily fluctuation. In Kabul, for instance, it may
be 30° at daybreak and rise to 100° by noon! Fog is practically
unknown in that crisp, dry air.

One of the trying features of the Afghan climate is the wind,
which has been known to reach a velocity of 110 miles an
hour; in the desert the people call this the "wind of 120 days."
In winter violent blizzards make life miserable for the poorly
clad villagers, many of whom lack shoes and sufficient fuel for
heat, and whose mud-roofed houses ooze melting snow as it
falls.

Afghanistan's main drainage systems are the Helmand
River, the Kabul River, and the Amu Darya, also known as
the Oxus. Of these three only the Kabul and its branches drain
into the ocean via the Indus River in Pakistan. The total
length of the Kabul is 380 miles, and it runs through fertile and
cultivated areas, but it is navigable only in spots and then only
for rafts and flat-bottomed barges. The Amu Darya rises in the
glaciers of the Pamirs and drains into the Aral Sea. Only
about 700 of the 1,000 miles of the Amu Darya, which forms
the boundary line between Russian Turkistan and Afghanistan,
flows through the latter, running at times through deep gorges
and navigable only for 550 miles. Afghans seem never to have
made use of their rivers and streams for trade and navigation,
although that may come with the development and modernization of the country.

In this latitude the Helmand is the largest river between the
Indus in Pakistan and the Tigris in Iraq. It has its source near
that of the Kabul at about 10,000 feet, and flows southwest to

the desert areas of Registan, then westward, and finally north to empty into the Hamun-i-Helmand, a lake on the Iranian frontier. The Helmand's total length is 700 miles, and with its various branches it drains the whole of southwestern Afghanistan.

These rivers of Afghanistan have a fascination and character entirely their own, unlike corresponding bodies of water in more lush and fertile lands where irrigation is in an advanced state, rainfall ample, and streams of all sizes and descriptions abundant, such as in Ceylon. Perhaps the overall barrenness and desolation, the paucity of forests and almost total lack of wildlife, give the look and sound of moving water a charm that one takes for granted elsewhere.

The Afghan government, with United States and United Nations financial and technical aid, has undertaken a major scheme for reclamation and irrigation in the Helmand Basin, a scheme designed eventually to transform the desert into productive orchards and farms.

I spent a night in the Morrison-Knudsen Company's resthouse on the site of the Helmand River Project, and met a handful of young American women and their children— families of American-trained Afghan engineers and officials connected with the Project. I was not prepared for the presence, in this wilderness, of compatriots of my own sex, and I was touched by the devotion and dedication of these American women to their husbands and the country of their adoption. Some of the wives had not been home to the United States for fifteen years, and the children of all of them had been born in Afghanistan.

The company had built a swimming pool and tennis court, and the radio beamed in programs of music and news reports from India, Pakistan, and Ceylon, but that was about all that these exiles could count on for distraction and relief. Because of the distance and nature of the terrain, not to mention the

scarcity and high cost of gasoline, they rarely got away from their own houses to meet with men and women of their own race, and these were few enough in Kandahar and Kabul.

As for the education of the children, the mothers had worked out a system of schooling along dual lines, American and Afghan, and I was told that in regard to religion, as the fathers were Moslem, the children would be free to make their own choice when they came of age.

Because of the presence of my young Afghan interpreter and guide, I did not feel free to question my hostesses too closely on certain aspects of their lives—on the question of social adjustments, political views, and so forth. They seemed happy enough, though I thought I detected a touch of wistfulness at parting, a nostalgia for home, for books, for contact with a

Kajakai Dam on the Helmand River

world which at times might have seemed to them to be very dear and faraway. And although for delicacy's sake we touched on it very lightly, I sensed a certain anxiety on another score: some of the children of these mixed marriages were girls, and Afghan society imposes strict laws governing the segregation of women, the majority of whom are obliged to wear the veil, or chadri, from the time of puberty on. This, however, is true mainly in the cities and towns. Country women and nomads seem to lead much freer lives.

But history is on the move, and many women in Kabul, the nerve center of political and social impulses for the whole country, have dared to discard the veil and show their faces in public. Great changes are occurring in Afghanistan, as they have occurred in other parts of the Middle and Far East.

Afghan farmers separating the wheat from the chaff

That night in the Morrison-Knudsen resthouse, I lay awake a long time, thinking of those American girls, of their attentive, gentle-spoken husbands, and the healthy, lively children—and I felt a great wave of admiration and respect for their pioneer spirit, part of the American heritage, but a spirit which asks more of its owners today than in an era when they had little or no choice about their way of life.

My thoughts went back to all that I had seen—Uzbek nomads with their camels and flocks; American exiles in this most unlikely of spots; dams, canals, highways; and only a few miles distant a half-buried citadel dating back to the Ghaznevid period. All these things coalesced to form a picture, part of which was the arid wasteland through which I had driven by jeep, where the only sign of life was an occasional encampment of untidy black tents and flocks of goats and fat-tailed sheep and the dust devils which, in that region, spring out of the ground and come whirling and twisting towards you with a ghostly motion that makes it easy to believe, as some Afghans do, that each spiral of dust contains an evil spirit, or djinn.

Driving through the Ghazni country another day, in pouring rain, I passed a nomad encampment in which it seemed that human misery must have reached its lowest ebb. The dry, eroded soil had turned to a sea of mud on which the flimsy tents seemed to float rather than stand. I had a glimpse of flooded interiors, of old people perched on boxes and bundles, while outside in the cold gray rain children swathed in sodden postins (goatskin jackets) kept watch over their dispirited flocks, and even the ferocious watchdogs were too miserable to give chase as we lurched past them, hub deep in slush.

On the whole, however, the Afghan nomad seems to lead a more idyllic life than his brethren in the city, and one is divided between admiration and envy of him, at times, as he follows the grass with his flocks, north in the springtime, south in the fall, taking his time, living in the clean, open air, unaffected by the strains and complications of the modern world.

An encampment of nomads, north of Kabul

CHAPTER FIVE
Nomads

The nomads of Afghanistan, or kuchis as they are called, are among the most interesting and picturesque segments of the population, of which they are said to constitute about one-third. Their exact number is difficult to assess, since they are continuously on the move, following the pastures north and south and vice versa, a way of life they have pursued through the centuries and which is not easily changed for another. Although they give an impression of Spartan frugality, and even of poverty, many are well-to-do, their wealth consisting of

44

flocks of camels, goats, and sheep, and some may own other property, such as houses, orchards, and crops.

These tribes, Hazaras, Uzbeks, Tajiks, Brahuis, and many others, are always jealous of their independence and mistrustful of officialdom. They fear, first, that too close scrutiny of their affairs may lead the government to press their sons into military service (compulsory for most of the male population) and thereby deprive the parents of potential domestic manpower; and, secondly, to an increase and implementation of taxation.

There used to be a time when the rulers of Afghanistan would forcibly transfer large numbers of people from one part of the country to another in order to break up or control the concentration of power of the big tribes, but this practice was dropped more than a generation ago, and the government now depends more on the arts of persuasion to get its ideas across. One of the most trying problems facing the government is the matter of educating the nomads, or tribes. Schools and teachers can scarcely be expected to trail along in the wake of seasonal migrations across the length and breadth of the land, and so far there seems to have been little desire for cooperation on the part of the kuchis themselves. Indeed, it is difficult to see how their footloose existence can be reconciled with a settled way of life.

The origin of these wandering tribes is more or less obscure, but it is thought that about the middle of the second millenium B.C., migrations of people gravitated from Central Asia and passed through Afghanistan, some to remain, others continuing on to India and Iran. Centuries after these early migrants came the Persians, after them the Scythians, the White Huns, and the Baluchis, to name only a few. All these people spoke languages which belong to the eastern part of the Indo-Persian group. It was not until the seventh century A.D. that people talking a different language appeared in Afghanistan—first the Turks, then the Mongols in the thirteenth century. The last important migration into Afghanistan was that of the Turko-Mongol Uzbeks, who established themselves as rulers of Afghanistan along the borders of the Amu Darya. These people are blood brothers to the present day Uzbeks of Soviet Uzbekistan.

There is an interesting corollary to these early settlers in the existence today of people who inhabit the southeastern province of what was once called Kafiristan, or the Province of the Infidel, a group which still identifies itself as descendants of the armies of Alexander the Great. Many of these people are blue-eyed and fair-skinned. They practiced a sort of pagan religion of their own until converted to Islam, when the name of the province was changed to Nuristan, or Land of Enlightenment.

Despite differences in language the way of life of those early-comers could not have been very different from that of the people who preceded them, or from those who were to follow. All practiced agriculture to a certain extent, others were pastoral nomads who lived in tents and raised animals for their livelihood as they do to this day.

There is an architectural form to the nomadic tent as there is to more conventional structures. The Turkic tribes to the north live in yurts, roughly dome-shaped, with a wooden frame covered with pieces of felt, whereas the tents of the southern nomads are pavilion-shaped and consist of lengths of black goat-hair draped over supporting poles. When traveling, the whole contraption is taken apart and loaded on to camels, along with pots and pans, bedding, babies, and old folk, and the caravan starts on its way—north in spring, to the verdant highlands of the Hindu Kush, and south in the fall, sometimes as far as Pakistan.

It is a great sight to see a nomad train on its way, the tall,

A nomad and his camels in southern Afghanistan

gaunt camels swaying forward in single file with the black tents and long poles strapped on their backs, flocks of goats and sheep straying on either side, herded by children and dogs, and the sound of a flute rising above the voices of the children and the tinkle of sheep bells. Occasionally one catches up with a nomadic wedding party. There was one I shall never forget. The bride, attired in scarlet breeches, long black shirt and headdress, her breast and forehead covered with gold, coin-shaped jewellery, marched spiritedly behind her young husband. She sported a long tribal rifle slung across her back and so did he. He carried a flute, upon which he played a snatch of tune as he walked, while she carried a tambourine. The girl was unveiled, with rosy cheeks and big black eyes, and she gave us a gay smile as we drew alongside.

We rolled down the window of the jeep and called the customary Persian salutation, "May you never be tired!" to which both responded, laughing, "May you never be poor!"

I made a point of stopping at some of these nomad encampments to talk with the occupants and take photographs, and always found them friendly and hospitable—something that could not be said for their dogs, which will often attack a stranger on sight and whose jaws look capable of taking off an arm or a leg at one bite. These great beasts, some of them as large as a small donkey, have their ears and tails cropped short to save these being bitten off by other dogs, or by wolves which still occasionally swoop down on the flocks at night. But in justice to those kuchi dogs it must be said that they are faithful to their masters and know where duty lies. I once saw a monster, halfway between a chow and a Great Dane in appearance, come charging down a slope in pursuit of a baby donkey which had wandered away from its parents and was in danger of being run over on the road. The dog approached the donkey on the offside and carefully nudged the tiny creature up the slope and back to its mama.

At one nomad encampment in northern Afghanistan, the head man, or chief of the group (by group I mean an encampment numbering anywhere from a single family to several families, traveling and camping together) posed for me with his youngest son in his arms. He begged me to concentrate on the child and not on *him*, for, he explained, he would spoil the picture because he had no teeth.

"But you have a fine son, Nam-i-Khuddar!" I said, invoking the name of the Almighty, as one must when extending praise. "Isn't that better than teeth?"

Hazara chieftain and
son pose for the author

He laughed and asked me to send him a set of false teeth from America, and when I suggested that he come to America himself, he replied that he would like to, but it would have to be by airplane, as camel-back would be too slow.

At this same encampment another nomad begged me for medicine for his sick son. The boy, about twelve years old, was led from his tent, and I thought that he showed all the symptoms of high fever. Through the interpreter I asked him whether he suffered any pain, and he looked puzzled. In response to further questioning it seemed that the word *pain* had no meaning for these people, though the boy kept putting his

A nomad woman displays characteristic shyness in front of the camera

hand on his stomach and making a grimace. I gave him aspirin, which I thought the safest thing under the circumstances, and told him to stay quiet and eat little until he felt better. He thanked me with a smile, and I reflected on the history of these people, of their reputation for savagery in war, their stoicism in the face of injury and hardship, and I decided that it was natural enough that a word common to us—pain— should appear to be missing from their vocabulary.

I was soon besieged by other members of the community— young men, old women, boys and girls. All declared they had something wrong with them—their eyes, their ears, swollen ankles, ringworm, fever. One middle-aged man displayed his leg, which had been broken the year before and had never been set. He complained that he found it hard to walk any great distance, and would I give him some of those white pills to make his leg strong and straight once more. I had learned from experience that it paid to carry a large supply of aspirin, and I doled it out, a tablet here and a tablet there, knowing that in such small doses it could do no harm even if it did no good.

The chief now asked me whether I would care to see the interior of one of the tents in which his people lived, and where I was invited to sit and rest while tea was being prepared for us. Inside the tent I found two young and pretty women crouched shyly in a corner. Although, as I have said, nomad women are not restricted to wearing the chadri, these covered their faces when my interpreter entered, and both refused to speak to us. The chief, his infant son still in his arms, followed us into the tent, chaffed the women good-naturedly, but made no attempt to force them into conversation.

Inside the tent the air was humid and heavy with the fumes of charcoal, goatskins, and the curious, all-pervading smell of roghan, the mutton fat in which they cook their food. The tent was about twelve feet in diameter and six feet in height, and housed an entire family including two baby goats and a litter of puppies. There was no furniture. Strips of goat-hide covered the floor, and a few pots and pans were arranged round the charcoal brazier in one corner. I noticed a fine rifle, worked in silver and mother-of-pearl, standing against the wall. Most Afghans go armed and all are excellent marksmen. They have a reputation for manufacturing homemade firearms of first-rate quality which they use to protect themselves and their flocks against wolves and other marauders, sometimes human, and to discharge the sacred obligation of the blood feud, or vendetta.

This shooting for sport and for food, together with relentless trapping and netting, probably accounts for the dearth of game and bird life generally. They even kill songbirds, and when I mentioned this to my nomadic host, he looked surprised and

Fat-tailed sheep,
outside Kabul

remarked that animals were created for man, and not man for animals, and that wildlife, as I called it, was meaningless. What counted were camels, donkeys, goats, and sheep. He made one exception to this, and described a bird which seems to have survived and which I had seen frequently along our route—a beautiful creature about the size of our American robin, but with a forked tail and iridescent plumage. My host called the bird ababil, and said that it was considered sacred by his people because of an incident in Islamic history. When Moslem Arabs were attacked by the Abyssinians, God sent aid to the Moslems in the shape of these birds, each of which carried a stone in its claws and one in its beak; every Abyssinian hit by the stones perished, thus assuring victory to the Moslems.

Conversation proceeded from the sacred to the mundane, and I learned that my host owned large flocks of goats and fat-tailed sheep besides the camels which I could see grazing a little distance away. I inquired about the matter of taxation, reflecting that the government must find it difficult to keep tabs on

these moving herds, and my host gave me a knowing smile and declared, in effect, that he paid as little in taxes as he could get away with.

The livestock tax in Afghanistan is in the form of a property levy which averages about three afghanis per head for all animals subject to tax, no matter what the size of the herd. The official rate of exchange is about twenty afghanis to the American dollar, and each afghani is subdivided into one hundred small nickel or copper coins called puls.

Although this nomad chieftain was to all intents and purposes a wealthy man, the living conditions of himself and his family could hardly have been more Spartan. The effect was enriched somewhat by the dress of the women, who wore long, bright-colored skirts and head-veils, and handsome gold and silver ornaments on their wrists, round their necks, and on their foreheads. I had been told that many of these ornaments were handed down through generations, and that some were believed to be of great antiquity and value.

Refreshments were brought into the tent by an older son of our host, and we were urged to partake. There was the usual hot tea, refreshing even on a hot day; yoghurt, called mast; and a dish of raisins and nuts. While we ate, my host answered my questions by saying that he was a Hazara, and that despite his nomadic way of life he owned a village in the Hazarajat in central Afghanistan. It was then I noticed his headgear, the round embroidered skullcap worn by Hazara men, and his tilted, Mongol-shaped eyes. If one were to live long enough in Afghanistan one would learn to distinguish a Hazara from a Tajik, and both from the Uzbeks and the Brahuis. Once, in the busy main bazaar of Mazar-i-Sharif, my guide pointed to a boy of about seven playing in the street with twenty others, and said, "That boy is not from Afghanistan. He comes from Pakistan." When I asked how he knew, he replied, "Oh, something about his eyes, something about the way he moves."

When we had finished our tea and thanked our host and the two shy ladies, who slid even deeper into their veils by way of reply, we stepped out of the tent and were starting towards the jeep, parked about fifty yards away by the roadside, when one of the encampment's huge watchdogs slipped its collar and came straight for us in snarling, bloodcurdling fury. We had nothing with which to defend ourselves, but our host's young son, who had brought us tea half an hour before, flung himself on the dog in a flying tackle that enveloped both of them in clouds of dust, while we—my guide and I—made a beeline for the jeep.

As we started away our Hazara chieftain called after us, "Come and see us again! I will shoot this dog. I will kill a sheep in your honor and we will spend the day in feasting and talk!"

CHAPTER SIX

The North-West Frontier – A Crucial Area

There are two possible points of approach to the story of Afghanistan: one to the north, where Russian territory thrusts down to the Oxus River, the other to the east, best known as the North-West Frontier, with a line of demarcation shown on the maps as the Durand Line. This line sets a broad belt of tribal territory off from Afghanistan proper to the north and west, and Pakistan and India to the south and east; and it is this approach which seems better for our purposes.

We should, however, bear in mind that while people still refer to this region (until 1947 one of the provinces of British India) as the North-West Frontier, it was in 1955 formally amalgamated with Pakistan, which now considers it an integral part of the western reaches of that country. For many of us who are unfamiliar with this part of the world, Afghanistan has too often been confused with the North-West Frontier, which,

55

while it is in the strict physical sense a geographical compo-
nent of Afghanistan, has from earliest times enjoyed a unique
and independent life of its own.

The picture is understandably confusing because the people
who live within the tribal belt and who are called Pathans are
also frequently referred to as Afghans, and vice versa. Actually
the difference is a simple one, and we need not go into long-
winded ethnic and genealogical details. The point to remember is that Pathans and Afghans are essentially of the same
stock—Turkish or Persian or a mixture of both, with strains of
Arab, Mongol, and Greek. The Pathan language is a branch
of the eastern Iranian group with two main dialects, Pakhtu,
which is hard and guttural, and Pashto, which is sibilant and
soft. The Afghans of Afghanistan proper speak both dialects,

Frontier guard

besides Persian, which is recognized as the language of the royal court and the government.

In religion the Pathans, like the Afghans, are Moslems of the orthodox Sunni sect, and they have a peculiar code of honor known as Pakhtunali, which imposes three obligations: to grant asylum to all fugitives (nanawatai), to proffer open-handed hospitality (milmastia), and to wipe out dishonor by the shedding of blood (badal).

This last practice still causes endless blood feuds originating in quarrels over women, money, or land. The Pathans of the North-West Frontier have a long history of such deadly feuds, tribe against tribe, family against family. The lives of women and children, however, are generally held sacred, and no blood feud can exist between members of the same family, since this would be looked upon as murder.

The Pathans have one rather charming custom: a man seeking sanctuary from his enemies may throw himself on the mercy of a neighbor by placing a bit of grass between his teeth and appealing to his host thus—"I am your cow!" Whereupon the host is bound by the Pathan code to take the stranger into his home and succor him even at the risk of his own life.

This Pathan code of hospitality is well illustrated by the following story. The Sultan Mahmud of Ghazni went hunting and wounded a deer with an arrow. The creature fled and took shelter in the tent of a humble shepherd, and when the Sultan and his entourage arrived on their horses, they found the shepherd standing at the entrance of the tent, barring their way. The Sultan commanded the man to produce the wounded deer, but he refused, declaring that since the wounded beast had sought refuge under his roof he was in honor bound to protect it at any cost. The Sultan blustered and threatened, his escort drew their swords, but the shepherd stood his ground, and in the end the royal party was shamed into going away without the deer.

In another story a gang of bandits attacked a village, whose inhabitants, men and women, rushed out to defend their homes—all but an old woman too decrepit to do anything. She stood in the door of her house, while her two sons engaged in the fight. The bandits were routed, but two of them, finding themselves unable to escape, forced their way into the old lady's house and begged for asylum. When her neighbors came after them and told her that the bandits had killed her sons, she replied proudly, "That is so, but these men came *nanawatai* under my roof, and no one shall lay a hand on them while I live."

Such stories may be apocryphal, but they are part of the Pathan's folklore and point up a way of life as it is practiced today.

The Pathan social organization, like the Afghan, is on a tribal basis. They are fundamentally democratic, and their passionate independence and frequent refusal to obey even their tribal chiefs, known as maliks, make them tough customers to deal with. The most important of the Pathan tribes are the Masuds, the Waziris, the Orakzais, the Afridis, the Mohmands, and the Usufzais. They are generally strikingly handsome and are renowned for their fighting qualities of which the British had more than a taste during the long period of British rule in neighboring India.

Centuries before the founding of the modern state of Afghanistan, about two hundred years ago, the region of the North-West Frontier, or the land of the Pathans, was for the most part uncharted country bordering on the then Indian province of the Punjab, with the river Indus forming a rough boundary dividing the wild uplands of the Khyber from the fertile plains of India proper. In those early times the North-West Frontier, with what is now Afghanistan, fell within the sphere of the ancient Persian Empire which stretched east and south to what are now India and Pakistan.

The Persian monarch Darius ruled over this whole area two hundred years before Alexander the Great came on the scene and marched his Macedonian columns of foot soldiers, cavalry, and camel trains down through defeated Persia, through Afghanistan, and on to the conquest of northern India, a prize which has fired the ambitions of conquerors from that day to this.

Coins, sculpture, and even glassware brought by the Greek invaders or produced by them during their brief stay in this region are still turned up by archaeologists, and some fine examples can be seen in the national museum at Kabul. It is interesting to note that, according to Sir Olaf Caroe in his splendid book *The Pathans,* Alexander and his armies had been completely forgotten in the areas of Persia and India through which he passed, until Greek and Latin records became available through translation into Arabic, and the great hero of ancient times was awarded his niche in the gallery of the Moslem world.

From earliest recorded history to the present, the lateral belt of territory known as the North-West Frontier has been the home of these highland tribes, some pastoral, some nomadic, living in scattered villages bounded by desert and mountain, and, until recently, lacking roads, railroads, airfields, postal services or telegraph, to say nothing of hospitals or schools.

Each tribe has been a law unto itself. When not warring with its neighbors, one tribe joined forces with another to conduct raids across the Indian border to pillage the farms and villages of the Punjab. They kidnaped rich Hindu merchants and held them for ransom, which, if not paid, usually resulted in the torture or death of the victims.

Raiding and looting have always been favorite forms of tribal sport and a lucrative means of livelihood. Until very recently these tribesmen recognized no law except the loosely organized control of the jirga. This was a council of elders which served as a kind of primitive parliament, ruling on such purely domestic matters as quarrels between neighbors, the settlement of blood feuds by payment of blood money, land disputes, and so on.

These Pathan tribes have been likened to the great highland clans of Scotland in feudal times, though it is doubtful that any Scot ever mustered the ferocity and fanaticism which has always distinguished the Pathan. Poor and illiterate, brave and proud, owing allegiance to no one, without any form of centralized authority or unity of purpose, the Pathans inhabited an area fated to serve in the nineteenth century as a sort of no man's land, separating two powerful rivals: the British Empire in India—and Russia.

Before the establishment of British supremacy in the middle of the nineteenth century, it was the Sikhs in the eighteenth century who exercised ruling power over the great tracts of the Punjab and the North-West Frontier as far as the Khyber Pass. The Sikh sect was founded by Guru Nanak (guru means teacher) as a protestant reaction against the polytheism and caste system of the Hindus, of which it is a branch. But it was not long before the Sikhs burgeoned into a martial clan, whose ambitious leaders turned their energies into attempted conquest of the tribal areas to the north, and of Afghanistan itself.

It should be remembered that the history of Afghanistan is inextricably bound up with the history of the North-West Frontier in its relationship to the past British raj and to the successors of that raj, the present nations of India and Pakistan.

It is necessary to mention a recent complication in the long and turbulent history of the Pathans. If you examine a map put out by the present Pakistan government, you will find it in direct conflict with contemporary maps published by the government of Afghanistan. The Pakistan version stands on an original British line of demarcation, the Durand Line, which places the whole of the North-West Frontier Province within the Pakistan orbit. The Pakistanis claim this region by right of inheritance from the British at the time of the founding of the two nations of India and Pakistan in 1947. The Afghans on the other hand have invested this same territory with a semi-autonomous character under the name of Pakhtunistan, or the land of the Pakhtuns, holding that since the inhabitants are ethnically of Afghan stock they have no place in either Pakistan or India, and furthermore that the relinquishment of British dominion makes the lines of demarcation quite obsolete.

There is something to be said for both sides in this situation, but what would seem to count is the majority opinion of some 5,699,000 of the Pathan inhabitants of the North-West Frontier

Native women weaving wool rugs on outdoor handloom near the Shibar Pass

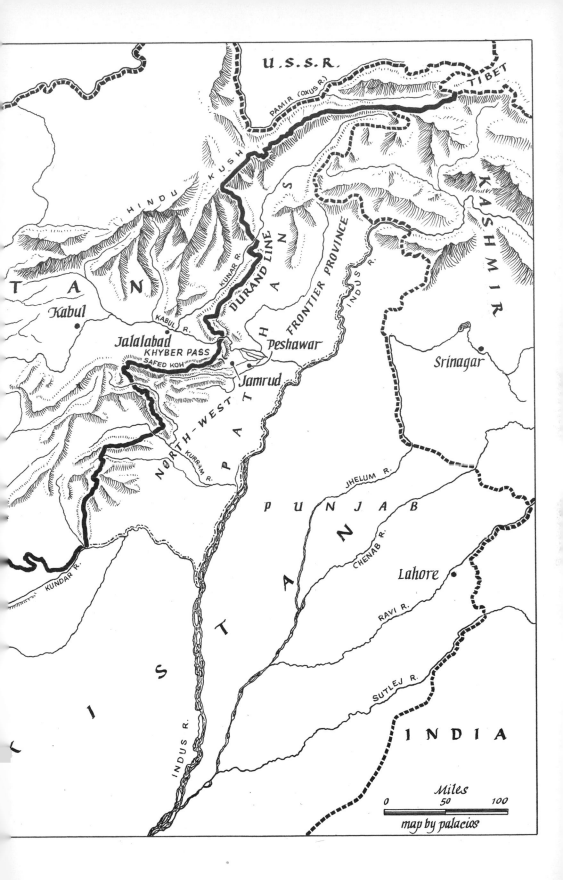

U.S.S.R.

TIBET

PAMIR (OXUS R.)

HINDU KUSH

KASHMIR

DURAND LINE

KUNAR R.

C H I T R A L

FRONTIER PROVINCE

INDUS R.

Kabul

KABUL R.

Jalalabad

KHYBER PASS

SAFED KOH

Peshawar

Srinagar

Jamrud

N O R T H - W E S T

KURRAM R.

JHELUM R.

P U N J A B

P A T H A N

T A N

CHENAB R.

Lahore

KUNDAR R.

RAVI R.

INDUS R.

I S T A N

SUTLEJ R.

I N D I A

K

Miles

0   50   100

map by palacios

themselves, and of these 99.5 per cent are reported to have voted by plebiscite in favor of joining Pakistan.

To go back for a moment to earlier history, it was only with the rise of British power in India in the latter part of the eighteenth century and the emergence of a recognizable Afghan state beyond the North-West Frontier, that this tribal area assumed importance both to Britons and to Afghans as a possible buffer state between them.

Not only were the British at that time concerned for the safety of their Indian subjects at the hands of loot-hungry and uncontrolled tribesmen, they were worried about Russian ambitions much farther away to the north, for by 1869 Russian influence had reached the shores of the Amu Darya on the northern border of Afghanistan. Britain, fearful of a Russian descent through Afghanistan in the footsteps of Darius, Alexander, Genghis Khan, and Tamerlane into her Indian Empire, decided to meet threat with threat, move with move. It is a long history of battle, advance, defeat, and retreat, of gore and glory, and if today at least one of the protagonists—Britain —is out of the running, geography and the insatiable ambitions of men still dictate the terms by which Afghan and Pathan, Hindu, Sikh, and Moslem must expect to live.

In 1893, with the Russians poised along Afghanistan's northern frontier and British power consolidated in the south, it seemed as if the ancient game of tug of war might at any moment burst into war without the game. It was in this atmosphere that Sir Mortimer Durand, then Foreign Secretary to the Government of India, journeyed to Kabul to try and negotiate an agreement with the Afghan ruler, Amir Abd-er-Rahman Khan, that would be satisfactory to all three powers concerned—to the Russians, the Afghans, and the British. In the tortuous and complicated deal which followed and which covered such matters as spheres of influence and lines of demarcation, the latter is what concerns us here. If you will take another look at the map of West Pakistan you will notice an irregular line wriggling from the southeast border of Iran to Pakistan in the northeast. This is known as the Durand Line, named for its originator. It is 1200 miles long and purports to set purely Afghan territory permanently off from that of the south and from the North-West Frontier, now amalgamated with Pakistan.

In 1879 a treaty was signed by Britain and Afghanistan placing Afghan foreign relations under British control, giving Britain control over the famous Khyber Pass and adjacent territory. This treaty was called the Treaty of Gandamak after the place where it was signed.

In order to maintain this control—vital, they believed, to the safety of India—the British went to work building roads and improving communications throughout a hitherto trackless waste. And they had to do it with rifle in one hand, since Western ideas of diplomacy, pacts, treaties and so on, meant nothing to tribesmen who had never been taught to read or write, but who nevertheless clung to an implacable sense of their own integrity and independence. It simply was not in them to be overawed by the appearance and high-handed behavior of strangers, no matter how benevolent, whom they believed had no business to be there.

The British built forts and garrisoned them with British and Indian soldiers, and it is interesting to note that the word *khaki* is said to have originated in this region and period. It derives from the color of the clothing worn by the Khattaks, another famous Pathan tribe, from which the British developed the familiar khaki battle dress because of its value for purposes of camouflage against this grim, bare, gray-green land.

The middle of the nineteenth century to the beginning of the twentieth was an era more at home in the arts of war than of peace, an era in which Rudyard Kipling was to write his ballad, "The Young British Soldier":

When you're wounded and left on Afghanistan's plains,
And the women come out to cut up what remains,
Jest roll to your rifle and blow out your brains,
An' go to your Gawd like a soldier.

The reference to tribal women may be unjust, but it does help to emphasize the people's reputation for unrelenting ferocity when faced with interference of their country and way of life. Much has been written of the courage and suffering of young British soldiers at that time, but nothing, or very little, is available to us of the suffering and courage of the Pathans, for they had no poets literate enough to immortalize their heroes. However, they left tangible memorials in their own fashion: the countless graves of their own dead and of the British,

A Turkoman smoking a water pipe

strewn for miles from the Khyber Pass to the borders of Baluchistan.

The whole period was for the most part one long, drawn-out fight between soldiers of the British outposts and hostile tribesmen who, operating on their own ground, armed with home-made rifles of deadly accuracy and with the murderous Pathan knife, often proved a match for their enemies. There is more than a touch of cynicism in another of Kipling's poems at that time, "Arithmetic on the Frontier":

A great and glorious thing it is
   To learn, for seven years or so,
The Lord knows what of that and this,
   Ere reckoned fit to face the foe—
The flying bullet down the Pass,
That whistles clear: "All flesh is grass."

A scrimmage at a Border Station—
   A canter down some dark defile—
Two thousand pounds of education
   Drops to a ten-rupee jezail—
The Crammer's boast, the Squadron's pride,
Shot like a rabbit in a ride!

With slight omissions the lines could have been written for the Pathan as well as for the educated young Briton sent out to pit his expensively acquired skill in war against men of his own age and of a race to whom fighting came as naturally as breathing. But if the British did not succeed in taming the North-West Frontier, they at any rate achieved their primary objective, which was the consolidation of a strong natural fortress in the territory which bordered directly on their Indian possessions. And if there is a touch of cynicism in Kipling's ballads, there is more than a hint of prescience in his great novel *Kim,* with its description of the fierce, hidden struggle between

British intelligence agents and Russian spies in the shadow of the Khyber Pass a generation ago.

I could not help being reminded of this when I saw that Russian gentleman get off the plane at Kabul, and perhaps, if he had ever read *Kim*, he may have had much the same ideas about my American fellow-passenger and myself.

It might seem as if those years of conflict between Briton and Pathan would have left a permanent poison in the memories of both, yet this does not appear to have been so. It must be remembered that it was an age in which both sides regarded war in one form or another as the only solution to any problem. The expression "cold war" had not been invented. Pacification by arbitration, when attempted, usually failed. The principle of temporizing and cooling-off periods, as we see it practiced nowadays, the good offices of neutral states and of institutions such as the United Nations, all were unheard of.

The Pathan code then, and in some areas today, was an eye for an eye and a tooth for a tooth, and in their struggles against the Pathans the British too often adopted this code as their own. While the more violent stage of the struggle continued, no holds were barred on either side. Perhaps the very intimacy of this passionate conflict brought a curious understanding of each other to Briton and Pathan alike, and with it respect and even admiration for the other's prowess and skill.

To quote once more from one of Kipling's ballads:

> But there is neither East nor West, Border, nor Breed
> nor Birth,
> When two strong men stand face to face, though they come
> from the ends of the earth.

Writers of the caliber of Sir William Kerr Fraser-Tytler and Sir Olaf Caroe, both of whom served in important administrative posts on the Frontier, speak with respect and sometimes

A friendly argument

affection of the Pathan tribesmen, and with more than passing
regret that Briton and Pathan should have met for the first time
on the field of battle instead of in the tent of friendliness.

If, for a moment, we can forget the more bloodthirsty and
romantic aspect of those times, the heroes sung and unsung,
and look at some of the other figures on the stage, we get
a glimpse of the beginnings of a more enlightened and humani-
tarian age. We find personalities such as Sandeman, Jacob,
Deane, Roos-Keppel, great Englishmen and great administrators who, as the tribal areas came gradually under some form
of centralized authority, bent their genius and their energies
towards the economic betterment of the tribes under their control. These men came to their jobs equipped with a first-rate
intelligence and a first-rate education which included fluency

in the languages, Persian and Pashto, of the people with whom they had to deal.

With the spread of British influence over the North-West Frontier, the opening up of roads and communications, the building of hospitals, schools, and irrigation schemes, the face of the North-West Frontier began to change. That did not mean that armed clashes were a thing of the past; they were not, any more than they are today, with the Pakistanis instead of the British in the driver's seat. It was not in the tribal character to accept change, no matter how beneficial, at the hands of a foreigner, no matter how well meaning, when such change was enforced by the iron hand in a velvet glove. However, some semblance of political order and economic improvement began to show where none had been before.

With the spread of education and inter-communication, a new class of Pathan appeared along the fringes of the tribal belt, and this to a great extent was brought about by the devotion and zeal of a dedicated Englishman, Roos-Keppel, working hand in hand with a distinguished Pathan, Nawabzada Abdul Qayyum. Together, they founded the Islamia College, now known as the University of Peshawar in Pakistan.

By 1930 the British had begun to extend a greater measure of self-government to India, and it was Nawabzada Abdul Qayyum who insisted that the North-West Frontier be included in the program of gradual emancipation. But the British Parliament in London believed that the area was still too small for such progress, whereupon Nawabzada is said to have pointed out that although a flea is a small creature, in his country people had found that it could be extremely troublesome when it got inside their pants!

However, as the Indian Congress Party—the party of Gandhi and Nehru, pledged to oust the British from India—grew in power, its example spread and inspired politically conscious Pathans led by two able men, Dr. Khan Sahib and his brother, Abdul Ghaffar Khan, the latter known as the Frontier Gandhi. These political groups wore red shirts and called themselves Khudai Khidmatgaran, or Servants of God.

At the time there seemed nothing paradoxical in such a party, altogether Moslem in faith, joining forces with the almost wholly Hindu Congress Party of India. However, the alliance was purely one of expedience, for as it turned out once the separate, independent states of India and Pakistan came into being, the overwhelming number of Pathans threw in their lot with their Islamic brothers in Pakistan. Only the future will tell whether this merging of the two will endure.

The present Afghan government, claiming blood brotherhood with the Pathans, insists that their amalgamation with Pakistan is ethnically and geographically impossible, and their maps testify to this belief. The Pakistanis on the other hand declare that since the amalgamation of the old North-West Frontier with western Pakistan is a *fait accompli,* there is nothing more to be said.

An open breach has developed between the governments of Afghanistan and Pakistan, and diplomatic relations between them have been broken off. While this may turn out to be a temporary state of affairs, it does go to show that impulses and ambitions rooted in the distant past can spring to life in our own day, with serious consequences for everyone concerned.

With the Pakistan-Afghanistan border sealed off, the Afghans lose their only access to the sea, via Karachi. Valuable exports of karakul, wool, nuts, and dried fruit are cut off, with corresponding economic loss. Goods and materials from the United States, destined for construction projects in southwestern Afghanistan, lie wasted on the Pakistan side of the border.

Even more serious is the plight of the nomads. Denied access to the winter pastures of Pakistan, they face starvation and possibly death for themselves and their flocks.

This leaves the Afghans with little recourse except towards their northern windows on the world via Russia. And so, with a spin of the wheel of history, Afghanistan finds herself once more in an ancient dilemma, caught between rival powers on her northern and southern frontiers.

Two women in chadris enjoy the sun by the river in Kabul

CHAPTER SEVEN
Women

Although there has not been to date a complete and dependable census of Afghanistan's population, the official estimate is set at twelve million, while unofficial observers set the total at no more than eight million.

The reason for this disparity in estimates lies in the enormous difficulty of carrying out a thorough count. The country is very sparsely settled, with the greatest density of population concentrated in the large urban centers such as Kabul, Kandahar, Mazar-i-Sharif, and Herat. For the rest, census-takers have to find their way to unnumbered tiny hamlets reached only by

73

footpath or pack trail, and in addition to these difficulties there is the major one of trying to estimate the number of nomads who are constantly on the move.

Besides these obstacles to accuracy, there remains the problem of ascertaining the number of persons in any given family. Traditional attitudes towards family privacy are strongly opposed to anything that smacks of prying, and it is considered an insult for an individual, even when on official business, to inquire too closely into the number of females in an Afghan household.

Anything resembling fraternization between Afghans and outsiders, Europeans, Americans, Indians, Russians, Pakistanis, is frowned on by Afghan officialdom, and this is especially true in the cities.

This attitude seems to be in direct contradiction to the time-honored principle of milmastia, hospitality, for which Afghans have always been famous. The reasons for this aloofness towards the foreigner are generally attributed to several factors: a deep-rooted suspicion and fear of spies, and the influence of the mullahs, the religious leaders and temporal heads of Islam in Afghanistan.

The mullahs have always been fanatically opposed to the presence of foreigners in the country, and probably with good reason according to their lights, for they have seen the influence of the Western world break down the barriers of reaction and bigotry in other Islamic countries—in Pakistan for instance, and, more notably, in Turkey under the revolutionary reform movement of Kemal Ataturk in the first quarter of the present century. Indeed, it was the powerful opposition of the Afghan mullahs which toppled the popular and progressive government of the Afghan ruler Amanullah, and which sent him and his family into exile in 1929.

Speaking from my own experience, I can only say that during my travels in Afghanistan I was the recipient of uncounted instances of kindness and hospitality at Afghan hands, in cities as well as in the country. At tea with a young Afghan family in Kabul, my host told me that he "could not wait" to have his wife and sisters take their place in a normal democratic society, and have them meet with men and women of other lands, just as he felt free to do.

"But we are obliged to go slowly," he said. "We cannot afford a repetition of what happened in 1929!"

He went on to explain that while Islamic law governs all Afghan society, it is the mullahs' interpretation of the Koran that is responsible for the plight of the women, and the mullahs are still powerful, a force for any government to reckon with. While the government itself, headed by the king and his family, are sophisticated, forward-looking men and women who would probably like to see the people throw off their archaic shackles, as the people of Pakistan and Turkey have done, the ignominious fate of King Amanullah is still fresh in everyone's memory, and the mullahs take care to keep that memory green.

It was amusing and a little pathetic to go to an American or United Nations social function in Kabul, one to which gentlemen were *not* invited, and to find one's host's door guarded by a couple of Afghan policemen with rifles, stationed there to make sure that no stray male tried to crash the gate. Then to find one's host banished, and, on entering the house, rows of gray, brown, or black chadris hanging on the coat rack, looking for all the world like the cast-off shadows of their owners. The latter, disporting themselves round the teacups, turned out to be as intelligent and attractive a group of women as one would expect to meet anywhere. It was always something of a

A young Afghan woman

shock to find them dressed, not in some exotic Eastern costume, but in Western-style dresses or suits, with nylon stockings and high-heeled shoes!

Strolling along the streets of Kabul on a windy day, one could sometimes catch a glimpse of a pair of toreador pants, or even well-cut shorts, fleetingly revealed under the chadri's drab disguise.

It seems impossible that this reservoir of feminine intelligence and vitality can be dammed up forever, but that the price of emancipation might turn out to be great, I can well believe. Let me give an instance of what I mean.

In Kandahar City, which, with Ghazni, is a center of mullah power and influence, I was invited by the governor of the province, a charming and cultivated gentleman, to visit a school for girls, and word of my impending arrival was sent well ahead. My Afghan interpreter and I were met at the school gates by a beardless young soldier armed with the inevitable rifle and bayonet. He greeted us with a smart salute and clicking of the heels, then motioned my companion to stand aside while he, the soldier, conversed with someone on the other side of the heavily barred wooden gates. I heard the voices of women, and an argument seemed to ensue, in which my interpreter laughingly joined. After a minute or two of this exchange, he turned to me with a shrug and said, "You may go in, but I must stay outside."

I protested and my protests were relayed to the ladies beyond and their verdict transmitted to me. "They say that *they* would have no objection to my accompanying you," said my interpreter, "but that I must remember that *this is Kandahar*."

There was nothing for it but for me to leave him kicking his heels disconsolately outside the gate, while I went in and heard the bars clang shut behind me.

Inside the courtyard I was greeted by a beautiful, dark-haired young woman—the headmistress, though she did not look more than twenty, if that. Dressed in a simple cotton dress, she wore a thin white veil over her head of gleaming black hair, and but for this touch, and an indefinable gentleness and dignity, she might have passed for an unusually good-looking European.

She addressed me in faltering English, then escorted me on a round of the school with its classrooms, playground, and so on. It seemed rather bleak and cold, without any of the cheerful touches and noisy high spirits of our own schools in the United States. I was allowed to take photographs of the

Three little girls at school in Kandahar

youngest pupils, tots from the age of ten down to four or five. All were dressed in little black dresses, all looked clean, and every one of them seemed to me to be of an exceptional prettiness and brightness.

When we had completed our rounds and I was about to leave, the young headmistress put a hand on my arm and asked me in a low voice whether I would take her picture, too. "But not here, not in front of the others," she added quickly, and led me around a corner of the building into a garden, where she posed against a sunny wall and I got a fine picture.

I said that I would send a copy of the picture to the school, but she shook her head. "Please do not send it here. We are not permitted to have our pictures taken. Please send it to my father's address."

I asked why I should be allowed to take pictures of the little girls but not of her, an adult, and she looked at me with big, lovely black eyes, then said with a smile, "Why? *Because this is Kandahar.*"

"And by that token," I said, "I was not allowed to bring that handsome young man in here with me?"

"Is he so handsome, then?" she wanted to know.

"Very handsome. And when I see him I shall tell him how beautiful you are."

She laughed, and as we walked back to the gate, she said, "One of these days things will be different, perhaps, even in Kandahar."

Afterwards, when I questioned my interpreter on the subject, he confirmed what I had already heard from other sources: that Kandahar was a center of mullah bigotry, hence the armed soldier at the gates of the school.

I had come to know my young guide well enough to risk asking a controversial question or two, so now, when I taxed him on the subject of women's position in Afghanistan, on their inferior status vis-à-vis men, their segregation and denial of the vote, he surprised me by the frankness of his response.

"It is all absurd, of course. It is only the older people and the mullahs who are responsible for this state of things. The young people want change. They want to see each other, just as in your country—they need each other."

"Even in Kandahar?" I asked slyly.

He replied with vehemence, "Yes, even in Kandahar!"

He went on to point out that while the position of Afghan women was hardly to be commended, according to Western standards, I should not run away with the idea that they were

unhappy in their homes, or neglected, or abused. On the contrary, most women enjoyed normal family life, and many of them wielded considerable influence in family and social affairs, even if behind the scenes.

I reminded myself that it was only in 1921 that American women achieved full voting rights in their own country, and French women as late as in 1944, and that there were still countries which prided themselves on their progressiveness,

The filmy headscarf of a factory worker in Kabul indicates a trend away from the traditional veil

← Chores are done by a stream in Istalif

among them the European states of Liechtenstein and Switzer-land, where women have not got the vote to this day.

The Afghan government knows its people and realizes that it must move with caution when trying to introduce changes in customs which have become ingrained in the public con-sciousness. As recently as 1960 there were severe outbreaks of violence in Kandahar as segments of the population, led by the mullahs, demonstrated against proposed changes in the status of women, and against what they regard as "foreign" influences generally. These demonstrations were said to be aimed as much against Russian activity in the country as against American and European.

It is always difficult for an outsider to get the truth of what is going on in the country, especially if the news happens to be bad or likely to inflame the public temper. Afghanistan has several newspapers—some with poetic titles such as Ittifaq-i-Islam, which means Concord of Islam; Tulu-i-Afghan, or Afghan Sunrise; Warengeh, Beam of Light, and so on—and the press is ostensibly free and uncensored. Nevertheless, one must remember that only a small percentage of the people can read or write, and are therefore bound to depend on rumor for their information.

What seems certain, however, is that troops and militia were called in to suppress the violence and to restore order in Kandahar, and that in itself is a sign that the government feels strong enough to use force to insure the public peace.

CHAPTER EIGHT

Social Customs

In the city of Mazar-i-Sharif in northern Afghanistan, I was invited by a young friend of my guide to eat lunch in the former's apartment overlooking the main street. Our host was a chubby, rosy-faced young man of about twenty. He was employed as a clerk in some minor official post, and this was his day off from work. His clothes were old but carefully darned, his apartment consisted of one small room with a minimum of furniture—no fan in summer, no heat in winter, but he had the poise and manners of a courtier. Already, out of his own meager pocket, he had ordered kebab and naan, and pots of hot tea from the best teahouse in the bazaar. When these arrived he waited on us himself, and we were soon conversing like old friends.

I learned that he was to be married to a cousin of his whom he had known since childhood, and that both sets of parents, hers and his, approved the match. Then he went on to explain something of the family and marriage customs of his people.

Marriage is generally arranged by the two families, the groom's family paying what is known as a bride-price to the girl's family, to validate the contract. The dowry which the bride receives from her parents is written into the contract and becomes the property of the young couple, to be inherited by their children. A man is not permitted to transfer property from the dowry of one wife to another wife or to her children.

When all the details for the forthcoming marriage have been settled, there is much visiting between the two families and gifts are exchanged. Guests arrive several days before the wedding, and the women of the bride's family, together with the groom's mother and sisters and their respective female friends, stay with the bride as sponsors, while the men of the groom's family act in the same role for him.

The bride is given a ceremonial bath. The groom's friends visit the bride's house and carry her gifts back to him. It is part of the ritual that everyone's hands are stained with henna, and the wedding festivities—singing, dancing, and feasting—continue throughout the night.

Loaves of naan, Afghan bread, ready for the market

One form of the marriage ceremony is called Aina Massaf, or "meeting in the mirror." On this occasion a mirror is placed in the hands of bride and groom, and in this fashion they see each other for the first time. The couple reads a verse from the Koran, the groom presents sweets to his bride, and the young women of the party dance in circles round the happy pair to the accompaniment of music on tambourines.

There are variations on the above procedure. For instance in some parts of the country bride and groom ride horseback through the village, accompanied by musicians and members of the wedding party, and sometimes the wedding procession takes place at dawn. I was awakened one night in Kandahar by the sound of drums and trumpets, and of guns being fired in the air. It was quite unnerving at that hour, until I learned that the uproar was not an insurrection but a wedding procession!

My friends in Mazar-i-Sharif went on to tell me that in Afghanistan the family is a patriarchal setup, and descent is traced through the paternal line. A married daughter is expected to transfer all allegiance to her husband's family, and a married man as a rule lives in his father's house, unless special circumstances, such as a job out of the country or the neighborhood, dictate otherwise.

The oldest male in the family has complete authority over the others, and as a rule a man will marry within the family group, such as with a cousin, as in the case of my young host. Under Islamic law a man is permitted to have four wives, but few can afford this rather dubious luxury, and as my friend pointed out with a laugh, he is lucky if he can afford one!

Under Islamic law divorce is easy enough. A man can divorce his wife simply by saying, "I divorce thee!" before witnesses. A woman, however, may not divorce her husband except on extremely serious grounds, and she can then claim alimony.

Street scene in Istalif

Afghan society tends to frown on divorce, and among certain tribes, the Hazaras for instance, it is not permitted.

Afghans bring up their children quite strictly. They are not permitted to cry or whine and are punished for lying or stealing. Oddly enough for such a reputedly fierce race, Afghans do not usually spank or strike their children, but rely more on lectures and appeals to the youngsters' pride, as deterrents to bad behavior. Some of the poor and uneducated discipline their children by frightening them with ghost stories and horror tales and threats of the evil eye. They will hang talismans round the necks of their babies, and they do not welcome praise of their children's beauty or health, since such praise is considered a direct invitation to bad luck.

If one should tell a parent that he or she has a beautiful son, one must immediately follow the words with "Nam-i-Khuddar!" (In God's name!) This invocation averts any evil influence which might be lurking around.

Certain people are suspected of having the evil eye, women particularly. Several times when walking through the bazaars of Afghanistan, I saw a passerby spit in my direction, and my first reaction was one of offense, until I realized that the spitting was merely a way of ridding the spitter of any evil influence which may have passed from me to him. Not very flattering, but to understand was to excuse. I know people of my own world who, when they spill salt, throw a pinch of it over their shoulders to avert bad luck, and others who would not dream of walking under a ladder, for the same reason.

In Afghanistan, as elsewhere in the East, great importance is attached to the birth of a boy, but the birth of a girl is considered something of a calamity, though I must say that in the Afghan homes where I was privileged to visit, the little girls seemed to be just as much loved and cared for as their brothers.

Afghans have a peculiar method of swaddling their infants. For the first few months of its life the baby is wrapped in cloth from neck to toe. Its arms and legs are bound with soft cords, so movement is almost impossible. This makes it easier to carry the child, and furthermore, prevents it crawling into danger, falling out of bed, or getting into mischief generally. I might say that all the children I saw running about seemed none the worse for this early strait-jacketing, and their elders, who had suffered similar early constraint, appeared in every respect as sturdy and upright as one could wish.

The brother-and-sister relationship in Afghanistan is a very close one, and in the case of orphans it is the brother who takes over responsibility for his sister, and it is to her brother that a girl will turn for advice and help.

Urban Afghan families, as well as other tribal people who live settled lives, usually occupy a single house or group of houses within a walled courtyard, or compound. Married couples have their own quarters within the main house, or perhaps a smaller house of their own, and it is generally the custom for the women of the combined household to prepare meals for all.

Afghans are strict conformists in all things and set great store by good manners. To be considered ill-bred is one of the worst stigmas that can attach to a sensitive Afghan, man or woman, and their children are brought up accordingly.

At mealtime, great restraint is used in eating. Knives, forks, and spoons are still comparatively rare in modest households, and people eat with their hands. The right hand only is used for eating, and then only the fingers, and considerable skill is required to keep them free of crumbs or grease. I watched very small children eating in this fashion, and was struck by their neatness and good manners. It is considered poor manners to ask for extra helpings of sugar for one's tea, and when the guest has drunk enough he is expected to turn his cup upside

Children in Mazar-i-Sharif were happy to pose for the author

down. However, if the host pours one another cup, the guest must on no account refuse to drink it. To refuse food when it is offered is to insult both its quality and one's host. Out of fear of this, in Afghanistan I found myself eating and drinking quantities which would have made me swoon at home. Often, as in the case of the young man in Mazar-i-Sharif, I was embarrassed by the open-handedness and prodigality of people whom I knew could ill afford it. But to have refused would have been a sin against good manners.

In Afghanistan boys and girls play together when they are young, but later they separate, girls to play with girls and boys with boys. When the girls are about twelve or thirteen they

Filling a teapot outside a chai khana

must put on the chadri, or veil, and are no longer permitted to go unveiled in public, although, as I have said, this custom shows signs of breaking down in the larger cities.

It was from my host in Mazar-i-Sharif that I learned something of the peculiar patterns of nomenclature of the Afghans. For centuries, an Afghan would be identified by the names of his grandfather, his father, and himself, each using a Moslem name, with the word "ibn" (son of) inserted between, thus: Yusef ibn Yusef Ali ibn Yusef Ali Khan. Khan is a kind of honorific, like the English title "Sir," indicating social position and prestige.

Nowadays there is a move towards standardizing family names, such as the adoption of a tribal origin as a family name, or the name of the place of birth, much as a Scotchman might use John o' Groats or McIntosh of McIntosh. Younger Afghans have developed the novel idea of using a name entirely of their own choice, usually with some sort of poetic or literary flavor, such as Mohammed Ali, Mountain-born, or Jan Mohammed, Man of the Wide-Open Spaces, and so on.

Forms of addressing people vary in keeping with the importance of the person addressed. There are two forms of the second person: shuma is commonly used for everyone, tu is used to children, lower-class people, and intimate friends. Oddly, it is the same word used in the same circumstances in India and in France.

There are two ways of addressing men equivalent to the English Mr.—shagali is the Pashto variant, aqa is the Persian. Merman is Pashto for Mrs.; Miss, in Pashto, is perleh, and in Persian is dushizeh.

So easy and informal had been the atmosphere of our luncheon in that little room overlooking the bazaar in Mazar-i-Sharif, that I felt relaxed enough to ask my host how he ventured to entertain strangers, and an unveiled white woman at that, in view of possible official disapproval. He replied, "You are a guest in my country, and for me that is enough."

"But what about those other guests in your country?" I asked. "The Russian engineers here in Mazar. I've seen them. Are you allowed to meet with them, to entertain them as you have me?"

He shrugged. "That is another matter. The Russians are the sole responsibility of our government, and we are not encouraged to fraternize with them."

Politeness forbade that I pursue the subject, but it set me to thinking and to recalling the many conflicting remarks and opinions I had heard in New Delhi and in Kabul itself. The presence and activities of Russian diplomats and technicians in Afghanistan were a source of continuous speculation among Americans and Europeans alike. We heard that these Russians were under instruction from their government to familiarize themselves with Persian and Pashto, to do everything to ingratiate themselves with local Afghans everywhere, to live as simply and as unobtrusively as the poorest of the people, and so to "show up" the American effort in Afghanistan—American ignorance of the language, American "indifference" to Afghan culture, American love of luxury, and so on.

The presence of these Russians, and there seemed to be quite a few, could be accounted for only as part of the Afghan government's policy, whatever that may be. They were certainly not there on private business; few foreigners are. As for spying, it would have to be something very special indeed and to call for genius, when one takes into consideration the difficulties of language and transportation, an extremely efficient government-controlled telephone system that links the country from north to south and from west to east, a vigilant and well-armed police and militia, and the fact that any stranger sticks out like a sore thumb.

The Afghans have had a long and bloody history during which they have tried to maintain their independence between two great empires, the British and the Russian, and they are now involved in a further struggle, which is no more than a continuation of the past.

My young host summed it up for me in this way:

"Americans criticize us for what they regard as our overfriendliness towards the Russians, but you must remember that they have been our neighbors for a long, long time, that they always will be our neighbors, and that they are very, very strong. True, we no longer have the British to bother us on our southern borders, but we have Pakistan, and *you* are giving aid to the Pakistanis, who do not like *us*!"

I glanced from the friendly, rosy face of the speaker to the window and the broad street beyond. It was lined with little

shops—food shops, fruit and vegetable shops, shops selling
crudely manufactured leather goods, others which specialized
in karakul skins and caps, and still others which displayed the
brilliantly colored chapans (the long buttonless coat worn by
men of the region). A few horse-drawn carriages rattled past,
a few bicycles, a ramshackle truck. Boys rolled iron hoops up
and down the street, women in chadris glided along like
ghosts, and little groups of bearded and turbanned men sat on
the platforms of the chai khanas, drinking tea out of gaily
decorated china bowls or smoking a big brass water-pipe as it
passed from hand to hand around the group.

It was a scene that spelled leisure, peace, people going
quietly about the business of living, offending no one and asking offense of no one. At the end of the street stood the most
sacred shrine in all Afghanistan—the tomb of Ali ibn-abi-
Talib, son-in-law of the Prophet Mohammed. Parts of this
beautiful building date to 1480 A.D. and the dome is covered
with shining faïence tile in blue, yellow, and green. Multitudes of pure white pigeons haunt the place, and, as I watched,
a flock of them rose and circled the air above the tomb, then
drifted slowly back to earth.

When, later in the day, I took leave of my young host, he
thrust a bunch of fragrant pink roses through the window of
the jeep, on to my lap.

"May you never be tired!" he said, in parting, and I
replied, "May you never be sad!"

The tomb of Ali ibn-abi-Talib in Mazar-i-Sharif →

An Afghan village

CHAPTER NINE
Village Life

An Afghan village is one of the most picturesque in the world, not only in the strict sense of the word, but because of the glimpse it gives us of a people and a way of life which has remained unchanged for centuries. In spring and summer brown adobe walls and mitered arches seem to sink luxuriously among groves of orange trees, apricot and almond, or acres of flourishing vineyards, for the Afghans raise fine grapes which are dried and sold as raisins, and which, with nuts and other dried fruit, form a large part of the country's export trade. These also help to extend the villagers' frugal diet of mutton, rice, and naan, the last a kind of bread made of whole wheat, pressed

96

into flat cakes and baked in the typical Afghan oven, known
as a tandur. This is a circular pit in the ground, lined with clay.
A charcoal fire burns at the bottom of the pit, and the wheat-
cakes are plastered on the sides of the pit to cook.

I have eaten this Afghan bread fresh from the oven and
found it delicious, especially when taken with a skewer of
broiled mutton, called kebab, and washed down with cups of
hot tea, with a handful of raisins and nuts for dessert.

Although Afghans raise fine grapes they do not manufacture
wine, nor do they drink it, nor, indeed, spirits of any kind. The
drinking of spiritous liquor is contrary to Islamic teaching,
though some Moslems in other countries seem to take the pro-
hibition more or less lightly. Not so the Afghans, with whom
one observes Islam in what is perhaps its most puritan aspect.

Naan fresh from
the oven is delicious

Since local water supplies are apt to be contaminated and wine is forbidden and there is neither coffee nor cocoa, the drinking of tea can be described as a national habit, as in China and Japan, and perhaps also in the British Isles.

Tea is not grown in Afghanistan but is imported from India and China and is usually of the strong black variety. Afghans drink it hot, with plenty of milk and sugar.

Every village and town has its chai khana, or teahouse, often more than one, and the fare varies according to demand. The chai khanas are the centers for gossip, exchange of news, refreshment, and rest. Occasionally one will boast a small radio which pipes in programs from New Delhi, Pakistan, and Ceylon. Almost every chai khana will have a small bamboo cage, hanging from a rafter, that houses a fighting partridge which lends its strident note to the hum of human talk.

Holding the little china bowl in both hands, sipping the hot tea, listening to the water bubbling in the big brass samovar imported from Russia, and hearing the people around me— even though I could understand little or nothing of what was being said—brought a sense of fraternity in the midst of the strangeness. To drink tea together, to break bread together, somehow made us all friends.

In one such chai khana near Tashkurghan in northern Afghanistan, as I sat drinking tea, a man wearing a purple-striped chapan and black turban emerged from a side alley, took up a position in the dusty little street below us, and began to gesticulate and speak in a loud chanting voice, as though inviting his fellow citizens to prayer.

My interpreter, seated beside me, explained that this was the village storyteller and that he was telling a story based on the life of the Prophet Mohammed. In a country almost 85 per cent illiterate, these village storytellers enjoy considerable importance, and the more animated their delivery the greater their appeal. This man, like most of his audience, could

Samovars are prominent features of a village main street
in northern Afghanistan

neither read nor write and had learned his art by word of
mouth as his father and grandfather before him. Asians generally seem to possess formidable memories, and generations of
illiteracy may have contributed to this power. They are forced
to learn by rote, and it sticks.

While our storyteller was talking, I studied the audience,
mostly men of all ages, seated on the little platforms outside
their houses, or leaning against the walls, or seated at the open
windows. A few small children in bright-colored clothes
squatted against the adobe wall across the street, and I could
see that their attention was about equally divided between the
storyteller and myself—a white stranger, a woman, suddenly
and inexplicably dumped in their midst.

"This is a big day for them," my interpreter murmured in
my ear, and nodded at the children. "For days now they will

repeat what the storyteller is saying, and compare notes about you—what you wore, the color of your complexion, and the manner in which you drank your tea."

When the storyteller had finished his tale, people flung coins into the street at his feet, and I suggested to my guide that we invite him to join us in a cup of tea. Our invitation was accepted with the charming Afghan bow, hand on heart, and we made room for him on the charpoy beside us. Conversation was conducted in Persian through the interpreter, who explained that I was an American and a writer of books. I saw the children's eyes grow round with interest. A jolly-faced Afghan seated near us asked if I would tell them a story—any story—but I excused myself by pleading a lamentable ignorance of Persian.

When tea and conversation came to an end and we prepared to pay our bill, the keeper of the teahouse—he did not look like a rich man—smilingly refused to accept payment. When we protested, he put his hand on his heart and bowed, saying that he considered us his honored guests. As we took our leave I could not help wondering where else in the world a total stranger would receive such open-handed hospitality, and from people whose very livelihood depends on being paid for their fare.

It was at this same chai khana, simple and unpretentious, with mud floor and thatched roof, that I noticed the beautiful red wool rugs and carpets that are made in northern Afghanistan. This type of weaving is done by women and children, sometimes an entire family working on one carpet. Each family has its particular design, handed down from generation to generation, rather like a European crest or coat of arms.

Since the average Afghan family, and certainly the poor, cannot afford much in the way of furniture, most of them sit on the floor, and if a room is too small to accommodate a cer-

Weaving a rug
on a handloom
in Istalif

tain carpet, one end will be rolled up against the wall to serve
as a sort of bolster for people to lean against. Rugs are used as
draperies for doors and archways, as saddlebags, and sometimes as decorations on walls, much as we use pictures.

Wood for building purposes and cabinet work is almost non-
existent, which accounts both for the mud and unbaked brick
architecture one sees everywhere, and for the devoted struggles
of peasants and farmers to promote the culture of trees, mostly

poplars which grow fast and can be planted from slips cut from the parent tree.

In the wooded areas to the north and northeast the people manufacture fuel out of charcoal, but the poor cannot afford to buy even that and are obliged to collect whatever they can—wormwood, weeds, sagebrush, and camel dung. Much of their time is spent in this pitiful search for the means to keep warm and cook their food. I have seen donkeys and camels piled high with great bundles of weeds of all kinds, and have wondered what could possibly be left for the poor animals themselves.

In common with similar situations in other parts of the East, it is this type of poverty with its resultant malnutrition and sus-

A village
grain store

ceptibility to communicable disease, that poses a major problem for the government. The Afghan government, helped by the World Health Organization, is working hard to eradicate or control such diseases as tuberculosis, typhoid, malaria, and others, but it is uphill work in a country where doctors and hospitals are few and far between, and where remote village communities still turn to the local snake-man for treatment of their ills. This is the other side of the coin, the reverse of the sunny, placid, tree-embowered village such as I have described at the beginning of this chapter. It is one thing to visit the village in summer when the sun shines and people can warm themselves in its rays, when the trees are in leaf, fruit budding, and flour bins full. It is quite another story when rain and snow fall and turn the streets to liquid mud, when roofs leak at every corner, and there is little fuel, and clothing and blankets remain wet from one day to the next.

Ignorance and poverty go hand in hand. Village barbers often act as dentists, pulling teeth or filling them without the boon of anesthetic, for they have none. Pregnant women call in a midwife for prenatal care and childbirth, with corresponding risks to the health and even the lives of mother and child. This condition is still widespread in many parts of the East.

In Afghanistan some sick people will turn to their mullahs for help, and are treated by prayer and incantation. Barren women pray for children at the local mosque. Such prayers are, as a rule, for the gift of sons. Wishful thinking and superstitious belief in magic sometimes work a cure, and if the patient dies anyway, it is accepted stoically as the will of God. Afghans, like most Islamic people, hold that all affliction comes from God, though blame is sometimes accorded to djinns and other evil spirits. The insane and the deformed are treated with kindness, since they are considered under the special care of Allah, the All-seeing, the All-merciful.

Enjoying rest and refreshment in a teahouse in Tashkurghan

This attitude was made vivid to me on one occasion when, pausing at the inevitable village chai khana for a cup of tea, I used the opportunity to take some snapshots of the village street and its inhabitants, most of whom seemed happy to pose for me.

While snapping pictures I saw, out of the corner of my eye, a figure seated against the wall of the chai khana, and a closer look revealed this to be a man of about thirty, shaped exactly like Humpty Dumpty, with a huge, oval, smiling face. He was clothed in the usual fashion of pantaloons, loose shirt, and turban, and I had not noticed him until this moment. So painful to me was his appearance with the enormous head and tiny shriveled limbs that I instinctively pretended that I had not seen him, and continued to take pictures of other subjects around me.

Later, when we were preparing to leave, my attention was attracted to him again, and I encountered a pair of bright, expectant eyes, and a wide and engaging smile. We left the village, and after a silence my interpreter inquired in a puzzled tone why I had not taken a picture of that man. I said that I was afraid he would have misunderstood and resented the attention as being a mockery of his condition.

"Oh no!" said my friend. "He *wanted* you to take his picture. You see, he doesn't feel sorry for himself, or different from the rest of us. Your leaving him out must have hurt his feelings."

There, in a nutshell, was the difference in reaction between one world and another, and I shall always reproach myself for having been so self-conscious when the victim of misfortune himself was not.

This Afghan wears the traditional chapan

CHAPTER TEN

The Afghan Personality

A great Englishman, the Honorable Mountstuart Elphinstone, writing in the early 1800's, evaluated the Afghan character thus:

"Their vices are revenge, envy, avarice, rapacity, and obstinacy; on the other hand, they are fond of liberty, faithful to their friends, kind to their dependents, hospitable, brave, hardy, frugal, laborious and prudent; they are less disposed than the

106

nations in their neighborhood to falsehood, intrigue and deceit."

Nowadays the reality that is a person is too often lost in a saturation of statistics and data, but in Afghanistan everything, everyone, still possesses a definite outline. You become aware of this whether you come to it through the winding reaches of the Khyber, or drift down from the skies on the dusty tarmac of the airstrip at Kabul. In the cities themselves there is less of the crowding that affects one in other parts of the East. Even nature ceases to crowd, and details are sharply etched, so that a boy's profile under the folds of his black turban becomes as unforgettable as the dark silhouettes of camels as I saw them resting like strange memorials among the graves of a Moslem cemetery outside Kandahar. There is no lushness in the loveliest of the gardens, no confusion in the landscape, and when the clouds boil upward into the incredible blueness of the sky, one has a quickened sense of something martial and grand, in keeping with everything that is best in these people and their past.

If one were to try and sum it all up in a word one would say "contrast." Contrast of hill and river and plain, between exquisite valleys and flat brown reaches of desert—or to use the more expressive word for desert, the Dasht. Contrast of character, of virtue and vice, terror and trust. There seems to be no halfway, nothing blurred, nothing gray. In the midst of an easy-going friendliness, a sudden thrust of fear.

I am reminded now of a morning at the city of Ghazni in southwestern Afghanistan. We—my Afghan driver, the guide, and myself—had stopped our jeep to fill up with gas at a roadside pump. My seat was beside the driver's, and because the day was warm the windows of the car were down, and while my companions supervised the filling of our gas tank, I amused myself by watching a segment of Afghan life being enacted before me.

A group of men in huge turbans and baggy breeches sat

against a further wall, smoking water pipes, while their women-folk, heavily veiled in the traditional chadris, crouched nearby, eyeing me intently from behind the embroidered latticework of their headdress. A boy was rolling an iron hoop, another taking pot shots into a tree with a slingshot. Two policemen with rifles strolled in the shade of the dusty poplars a little distance away.

My attention focused on a pair of donkeys advancing up the street towards me. Across their backs was laid a charpoy, or string bedstead, and on this lay the figure of a man wrapped in a blanket, evidently ill or hurt. Two other men were trying to make the donkeys keep an even pace so as not to dislodge the bed. The rickety cortege passed me and pursued its erratic course out of sight, and then I became aware of a figure standing close beside me at the window, so close in fact that his sleeve brushed mine, and I found myself looking into the face of an old man with a shining white beard and the hieratic, hawk-like features of a true Pathan. He did not speak, but slipped one hand into the bosom of his shirt and began to draw out something that looked like a stone spearhead or arrow-head, about six inches long, and for a moment I thought that this must be something he wanted to sell me.

Now, Ghazni is the site of a great center of civilization in the past when, under the Turkish adventurer Mahmud, the city boasted some of the most beautiful buildings of the time, and was the home of the poet Firdausi, known as the Persian Homer. Later, Alauddin, described as the World Burner, sacked the city and set fire to it. These were not men to do things by halves, and history describes how seventy thousand human beings were put to the sword or burned to death in a holocaust which lasted seven days and seven nights. Everything was destroyed except the tomb of the great Mahmud himself, and the two magnificent towers of victory erected by him on his return after the triumphant conquest of the Punjab in India in 1026.

It was Mahmud's tomb and the rubble of the ancient city that I had visited the day before, hoping that I might chance on some tiny souvenir among the stones and weeds. So, when the old man at my jeep window produced from his shirt what I took to be an object of possible interest, I instinctively put out my hand to receive it. At that moment two younger men appeared, took the old one by his elbows, and quietly led him away. It was done quickly, unobtrusively, and, disappointed though I was at not being allowed to at least examine something that might have been interesting, I remembered that casual peddling was not common in Afghanistan, so decided

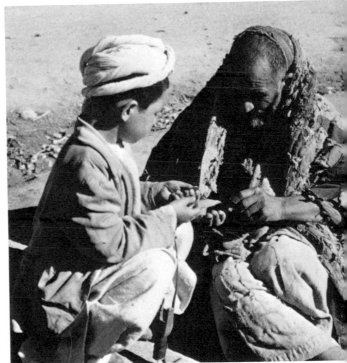

A small boy
and a blind village
beggar examine a coin

that the young men probably acted out of fear lest their old friend get into trouble for harassing a foreigner.

I thought no more of the incident until my guide and the driver were back in the jeep. We were starting away from the gas pumps when I spied my old man moving up the street, escorted not by the two young men who had eased him away from my window, but by the two policemen with bayonets fixed!

I pointed this out to my guide and told him what had taken place at the window, whereupon he seemed perturbed and made me give a detailed description of the object which the old man had partially drawn out of his shirt. "He was probably trying to sell it to me," I suggested, but my friend shook his head. "Peddling is not done hereabouts. I don't know . . . he may have been one of those crazy fanatics. We still have

Outdoor barber-shops are a common sight on the streets of Kabul

some, you know. They hate foreigners, women especially, and unveiled women in particular."

Incredulous, I asked, "Do you believe that that thing he had in his hand was a knife, and that he intended to stab me with it?"

My young friend looked more troubled than ever. "I don't know. I didn't see it, so I cannot say. The government does its best to control such people, but we can't account for all of them. However, from now on we will keep that window closed, if you don't mind."

I shall never know what was at the bottom of that incident, whether or not I had come within inches of being knifed. I had heard of other instances of foreigners being attacked by fanatics whose creed teaches them to destroy the infidel and thus insure themselves a passage to heaven. My own feeling is that these "fanatics," fearful lest their immemorial way of life and their religion be menaced by alien influences, act out of nothing more mystical than plain dislike and mistrust of the stranger.

Let me balance the account by describing another incident which occurred in about the same neighborhood, when, strolling down a village street, I was caught in a brisk shower of rain without coat or umbrella, and with every prospect of being drenched to the skin. I had left the jeep at the other end of the village street and as I started back towards it I came alongside the open door of a little house which framed a charming picture: an old man, white bearded and heavily turbanned, squatted on the floor with a small boy curled beside him. The old man held a copy of the Koran open on his knees and was reading aloud from it, while the child repeated the lesson with an air of profound gravity and concentration.

The Koran is written in Arabic, the language in which it is committed to memory even by those who do not speak that language. Despite the downpour, I could not help pausing to take in the little scene and to listen to the cadence of the old man's voice. Then he glanced up and saw me, pointed to the dripping sky, and motioned me to come in and shelter under his roof. I did so and sat on the floor near them. The lesson continued until the rain let up and I rose, and, bowing my thanks, received from each of my hosts a smile and a bow in return.

There is a peculiar charm in Afghan manners, a mixture of formality and warmth. Two gentlemen meeting on the street will bow to each other, hand on heart, then embrace. Their handshake is firm and prolonged, and they manage to make you, a stranger, feel as if you were doing them the greatest honor if you should ask a simple favor.

A small Afghan boy
in Charikar

CHAPTER ELEVEN

The Past
and the Conquerors

Every nation in every age has its great men, the adjective denoting qualities peculiar to the history and character of the people. In the Western world, as much importance attaches to great scholars and poets as to soldiers and statesmen, so that the Greeks have Socrates and Agamemnon, the French Voltaire and Napoleon, the English Shakespeare and Wellington, the Americans Walt Whitman and Lincoln. If we want to include Russia, we can say that they have Dostoevsky and Pushkin and Peter the Great.

In the countries of the East, greatness has until recently enjoyed a somewhat different connotation. Vast illiterate populations have had no means of assessing the qualities of any poet or philosopher who might have been among them, and lack of communication—of newspapers, magazines, radios— made it difficult if not impossible for the great mass of the people to judge the worth of leaders to whom they had, willy-nilly, to submit.

In these societies, greatness was merely the power of the current ruler to impose his will, and since the power was more often than not omnipotent, and possibilities for its abuse unlimited, greatness came to be associated simply with strength. The more remote the country geographically, the more impoverished and backward the people, the "greater" the personality of the ruler. Hence the suffix "Great" to such figures as Darius I of Persia, Peter of Russia, Alexander of Macedon, and so on.

Afghanistan has had its gallery of great men, and, given its geographical position and the headstrong character of its people, it seems only natural that, for them, greatness has meant martial and dictatorial attributes, and often downright bloodthirsty ones. These were the attributes of warriors but in many cases of entrepreneurs also, for they kept the trade routes open to permit the passage of silk caravans from China through the Pamirs and across the Hindu Kush mountains into India.

It was in the middle of the tenth century that a Turkish slave named Alptigin founded a line of conquerors, the most renowned of whom was Mahmud of Ghazni, also known as Mahmud the Iconoclast, or Image Breaker. Mahmud extended his dominion from Afghanistan to the Punjab in India, and beyond. He used the booty accumulated by these conquests to adorn and enlarge his capital at Ghazni, where he built a beautiful mosque to commemorate his victories, and endowed seats of learning which attracted poets and scholars from other parts of the world.

Perhaps we can call Mahmud great, since he seems to have combined the genius and daring of a military adventurer with an appreciation of art and learning. It must be remembered that his was an age when unchallenged power vested in one man brought forth the full uninhibited qualities of the man, bad with good, and in Mahmud's case it left an echo which still rings in Afghan hearts.

A view of the gardens at Istalif

In the thirteenth century we come to a name famous and infamous in history, that of the Mongol chieftain Genghis Khan, who with his hordes penetrated deep into Afghanistan and left death and ruination in his wake. The greatness of Genghis seems to derive almost entirely from a capacity for savagery for savagery's sake. Conquest meant not only the massacre of countless men, women, and children; it also meant the destruction of their homes, their flocks, and their crops, so as to make sure that the few who might chance to escape the sword would die of starvation.

Genghis had a descendant, Tamerlane, A.D. 1336, who seems to have inherited his ancestor's taste for blood. With his army, he passed through Afghanistan into India and sacked Delhi, equaling if not surpassing the example of Mahmud of Ghazni and of Genghis Kahn himself.

A truly illustrious name on the long list of conquerors and freebooters who left their mark on Afghan soil was Zahir-ud-Din-Muhammad Baber, yet another descendant of Genghis Khan, and founder of the great Mogul Empire of India. Baber conquered Afghanistan and made Kabul his capital. Thence he descended into India, where he defeated Ibrahim Lodi, the

The tomb of Baber

Afghan king of Delhi, and made himself master of the realm.

Baber was a military leader of the first order, a brave and resourceful soldier, but he was also a cultured gentleman, a lover of literature and poetry and nature. His memoirs give one a witty and discerning picture of the life of his time and are a pleasant relief from the long chronicle of woe and desolation left by his predecessors.

Baber loved Afghanistan, the land of his adoption, and he lies now under the beautiful chenar trees in the Bagh-i-Baber, Garden of Baber, just outside the city of Kabul. The grave is simple and unpretentious, and when I visited it a few old men were saying their prayers beside it, and a group of children were playing under the trees. It occurred to me that this was the ideal resting place for a great warrior who could write lovingly of the look of the countryside in springtime, and of the sound of running water and the scent of flowers.

Baber was the grandfather of Akbar "the Great," a contemporary of Queen Elizabeth I of England, and the best known of the Indian emperors. It was Akbar's engineer who built the first road through the Khyber Pass.

Nadir Shah, King of Persia from 1736 to 1747, was a later invader of Afghanistan. Like his predecessors, he was on his way towards the conquest of India, which he achieved at the head of his Persian troops to the accompaniment of the usual bloodshed, chiefly among the wretched citizens of Delhi.

In this campaign Nadir gained possession of fabulous amounts

Afghan boy

of loot, including the famous Peacock Throne and the Koh-i-noor diamond, which is the most precious of the gems set in the royal crown of the rulers of the British Isles. Nadir was eventually murdered by some of his own soldiers, but not until he had lapsed into insanity and imposed dreadful barbarities on his victims, among them his own son. This was the provocation, no doubt, that led to his end.

It can be seen that until about two hundred years ago the history of Afghanistan was mostly that of an unlettered, unfederated land of tribal people, some nomadic, others living in the characteristic walled and fortified villages still in existence today. It was an era of petty chieftains, who, when not fighting among themselves, were trying desperately and unsuccessfully to fend off powerful invaders from their frontiers.

It was an age of unceasing strife between one short-lived dynasty and another, of brother against brother and puppet against puppet. A history of bloodshed, of ingenious and terrible tortures inflicted by victors on vanquished, and—above all—the even more terrible and eloquent silence of multitudes of helpless people who had no share in the spoils and who asked for nothing more than to be left in peace.

It seems strange, but it is nevertheless true, that an age and a people which thought nothing of putting out a man's eyes or flaying him alive or dismembering him limb from limb, could still produce poets such as Khushal Khan, a tribal chieftain of the seventeenth century, who wrote lyrically of life and love and the innocence of nature:

> As the rose blooms, so it also fades away,
> As the short life of the rose, so is mine counted;
> Still is death better for me than life itself,
> Since my soul I have abandoned for the love of the beloved.

CHAPTER TWELVE

Religion

Alien invasions often bring something of value which is re-
tained and assimilated by the vanquished long after the invader
has gone his way, or his power has petered out with time.
Sometimes the thing of value is a new religious belief and a corresponding shift in the spiritual insights and social mores of the
very people who fought and bled to preserve their own.

In Mexico at the time of the Spanish Conquest, the Mexi-
cans first resisted fiercely, then accepted the Christian ideal in
place of the totem worship of their forefathers. Modern Mexico
is the result of a dual victory: of bloody victory imposed by the
sword and spiritual victory gained by the adoption of a gentler
creed.

In India, Ceylon, China, and Japan, the discipline and self-
abnegation preached by Gautama Buddha scored a bloodless
victory over polytheistic superstition, and penetrated into Afghanistan to glow briefly and brightly under the shadow of the
Hindu Kush. Today, if you go to the valley of the Bamian, you
can see what is left of the marvelous center of Buddhist thought
and teaching, established there in the fourth and fifth centuries
B. C.

119

The Bamian River runs turquoise colored between cliffs of rose- and vermilion-colored rock, into the walls of which are carved colossal statues of the Buddha. I have crawled along the perilous approach, cut into the ledge, and emerged on the Buddha's head, there to sit and gaze upon the lovely landscape, which could not have changed much since his time. Below me was the village of Bamian with its mud walls and quadrangles, fields of wheat and the pale green of poplar trees, and distant, tiny forms of men, women, and children, of camels, horses, and sheep, all going about the business of living and working in the fashion of generations past. Afghanistan is still a long way from mechanized farming, and the people I saw working in the fields were using primitive hand tools and their plows were made of sharpened wood drawn by oxen or mules.

In the ceiling above my head were remains of ancient frescoes, paintings of angels and bodisattvas and lotus flowers. Under me was the great torso of the Buddha, and here the word great comes into its own. The whole concept was one of grandeur, of a serene and magnificient spirit brooding over this ancient landscape, surviving centuries of blizzard, earthquake, and flood, and, what is more, surviving defacement at the hands of Moslem invaders of the seventh century. These poured through the Bamian valley intent on conquest and the spreading of their own faith of Islam, one of whose tenets is that man must not create images unto himself, and that to raise an image to one's God is to be an idolater, deserving defacement and death.

Bamian had once been a place of pilgrimage for priests and scholars, and there was a time when the whole site was a gigantic monastery, with cells cut into the cliff sides. To this day the walls and ceilings of these countless cells are stained with the smoke of fires which have been dead more than five hundred years.

The valley of the Bamian →

The mammoth Buddha surveys the valley of the Bamian

At the time of its greatest glory Bamian was a city unto itself, where scenes of splendor were enacted during the religious festivals. Golden banners floated in the breeze, brilliantly robed priests and their acolytes moved in huge processions to the feet of the statues, and the air throbbed with the beating of drums and cymbals and the shrilling of flutes.

In that day the statues were painted in vivid colors touched with gold, and when the western light fell on them they must have glowed with unearthly magnificence against the background of colored rock, and dazzled the eyes of the crowds assembled to worship at their feet.

The pomp and splendor are gone, but the figures survive, part of the features cut away by fanatics of another creed and another age, but it seemed to me that as long as they stand they will symbolize humanity's ideal of greatness: gentleness, serenity, and compassion.

From where I sat on the head of the mighty Buddha of Bamian I could see a small rose-colored hill crowned with ruins which once had been the original fortified city of Bamian. When Genghis Khan in the thirteenth century, on his way south from Bactria, invaded this delectable valley, he laid siege to the town, and his son Mutufer was killed in the battle. Out of revenge, Genghis leveled the city and slaughtered the populace, sparing no one.

Genghis Khan had a grandson, Kublai Khan, at whose court the Venetian traveler Marco Polo visited, and of whom Samuel Taylor Coleridge wrote the poem "Kubla Khan," which begins:

> In Xanadu did Kubla Khan
> A stately pleasure-dome decree
> Where Alph, the sacred river, ran
> Through caverns measureless to man
>   Down to a sunless sea.

Buddha preceded Christ by five hundred years, and the next great religious figure after Christ was the Prophet Mohammed, which means *praised.* Mohammed was born in Mecca, Arabia, about the year 570. He was the son of a rich merchant, and it was not until he was forty years old that he began to have visions and believed himself to have been singled out by God to be his prophet on earth.

It was Mohammed who founded the Islamic faith, which teaches, among other things, that people must pray five times

The great Moslem shrine in Mazar-i-Sharif

a day, give alms to the poor, and abjure usury. The Islamic calendar starts at the time of the Hegira, or flight of Mohammed from Mecca, where he was being persecuted by his enemies. In 622 he arrived in Medina, also in Arabia, and this became his headquarters and the center of Islamic zeal.

Mohammed's teaching ran into strong opposition from pagan Arabs, as well as from Christians and Jews, but in the end Arabia was converted to Islam. Mohammed considered himself as the last of the prophets, and as a successor to Jesus

View from the Buddha's head

Christ. Moslems have never recognized the divinity of Jesus, though they revere Him as a great prophet, as they do Moses.

Islam was carried to Afghanistan by a succession of Arab invasions, and it has since been the main unifying force in the country, as it is throughout the Middle East. Islam is not only a religion; it is also a way of life, and it governs Moslem society in almost every phase. As the Afghans themselves belong to this militant proselytising faith, they will not tolerate missionaries or priests of another religion, and these are not permitted to stay in the country.

However, people of other religions—Christians, Jews, Hindus, Sikhs—are allowed to practice their rituals in private and are not interfered with, although until recently the small Jewish community in Afghanistan was compelled to pay a head tax and to wear a distinctive form of dress.

The militant nature of Islam seems to fit well with the fiery character of the Afghan people. Whenever Afghans have risen to defend their soil they have done so in the fanatical belief that they were at the same time defending their faith. All wars with them have been in the nature of holy wars, or, as they call it, Jihad. It is this spirit as much as anything that has given them their reputation for utter recklessness and disregard for life. It is one of the tenets of Islam that a Moslem who kills an infidel goes straight to heaven. What terrors, then, can death hold for the Faithful? Obviously, none.

CHAPTER THIRTEEN

Modern Rulers

The establishment of British power in India was followed by
two centuries of skirmishing, of raid and counterraid, of direct
armed intervention and the setting up of puppet rulers in
Kabul. There were, of course, intervals of peace and good relations, notably towards the latter half of the nineteenth century, when the British found it possible to come to terms with
two hard-headed and able Afghan rulers—Abd-er-Rahman
Khan and his successor, Habibullah Khan.

The latter was a man to whom the British owed much, since,
in accordance with his treaty with them, he kept his fire-eating
subjects in check and maintained strict neutrality during the
first World War. This was something of a feat when we remember that his coreligionists, the Turks, were fighting on the German side, and Afghan tribesmen were itching to seize this opportunity for paying off old scores against their traditional
enemy, the British raj.

Habibullah's loyalty to his pledge, together with what some
of his subjects regarded as his treasonable tolerance of the

British, resulted in his murder at the hands of fanatical nationalists in 1919, and his son Amanullah mounted the throne. This brings us to a definite break in the long and familiar pattern of Afghan history, for with the new ruler a new era came to Afghanistan.

Amanullah's first act on ascending the throne was to declare war on the British. This was done as an attempt to disavow his father's discredited policy and to insure his own position in Afghan eyes. He invaded the Indian frontier and was defeated and he and his army thrown into ignominious retreat behind their own lines. However, peace was eventually concluded, and for their part the British agreed to respect Afghan territory and to recognize its complete independence, whereafter Amanullah felt free to turn his energies to other fields.

He had traveled in Europe and the Middle East and had been greatly impressed by the civilization and high standards of living of those countries in comparison with his own. He was particularly impressed with Turkey, whose great emancipator, Kemal Ataturk, had completely transformed Turkish society from that of a sort of Arabian Nights' tale into a modern state.

Ataturk had given his country a constitution; he had built schools and hospitals, expanded trade, and brought Turkish women out from behind the veil. In short, he had put Turkey on the map with the Western world. Like Afghanistan, Turkey is an Islamic country, and King Amanullah decided that what Kemal Ataturk could do, *he* could do.

Amanullah was young and impetuous and perhaps a trifle silly. He should have understood his own people better, and above all he should have taken into consideration the possible reaction of the mullahs with their ever-ready rallying cry: Religion in danger! The mullahs, always jealous of their power and prestige and invincibly opposed to any change that threatened their position, were scandalized by their ruler's behavior.

Amanullah returned from his travels fired with enthusiasm for reform and the rapid modernization of his country and people. One of his first moves was the abolition of the chadri, or veil, for the women. His own queen and the ladies of his household set the example by appearing in public without their veils, and, not content with this, he went around himself wearing Western dress and compelled the Loe Jirga, the august and dignified Council of Elders, to appear before him clothed, not in their traditional Afghan costume, but in frock coats, striped pants, and top hats. This lent a Gilbert-and-Sullivan touch to a situation that was far from comic under the surface. The whole country was smoldering with revolt, fanned by the mullahs and nourished on ancient fears and suspicions of anything that smacked of the new and the strange.

Amanullah came of a race and a lineage accustomed to having their own way. His ancestors had been omnipotent rulers over a turbulent people who, in their turn, were not

averse to taking the law, or what passed for it, into their own hands. He should have given thought to his country's history, stained with the crime of regicide, of which his own father had been a victim. But carried away with enthusiasm and the desire to go down in history as an emancipator as great as, if not greater than Kemal Ataturk, Amanullah continued to rush his well-meaning but unwelcome reforms until his subjects, egged on by the mullahs, rose against him. Revolution broke out, and the king and his court were forced to flee. They were lucky indeed to escape the fate of their predecessors and a similar fate which was to overtake the next legitimate king.

There is one amusing note to the story of Amanullah's flight. A young noble of the royal household made his escape from the country with two of his most cherished possessions—a beautiful and valuable carpet and an equally beautiful and valuable horse. They had to cross difficult country, part of it deep in mud. The young man's horse foundered, and fearful

A wet winter day
on Jadee Maiwand Avenue in Kabul

of losing not only his treasures but perhaps his own life, he hit upon the ingenious idea of spreading the priceless carpet on the ground and leading his horse over it, repeating the procedure until the going improved and he was able to mount and ride away, carrying the bedraggled carpet as a memento of his escape.

Amanullah's flight in 1929 threw the country into confusion, and the throne was soon usurped by a swashbuckling character known as Bacha Saquao, which means Water Carrier's Son. Bacha ruled stormily for eight months or so, then he, too, was liquidated, and the new king, Sirdar Nadir Shah, mounted the throne. This Nadir Shah should not be confused with the Nadir Shah mentioned in a previous chapter. Afghan names are frequently duplicated in history, and in this case they are separated by one hundred and fifty years.

It was under Nadir Shah that Afghanistan, for the first time in its history, became a constitutional monarchy in the year 1931. Nadir Shah was a wise and able monarch, but he was destined to rule only three years, when he, too, met death at the hands of an assassin—a young man who, it is said, was paying off a blood feud against the person of the king. King Nadir was succeeded by his son, Mohammed Zahir Shah, the present ruler of Afghanistan.

This brings us to the present time, to an Afghanistan which has changed drastically since the days of Abd-er-Rahman Khan and Habibullah Khan, changed even from the time of Amanullah, who would smile a trifle wryly, I suspect, could he return to find changes which he himself had hoped to bring about forty years ago.

Modern Afghanistan is recognized as a constitutional monarchy under King Mohammed Zahir Shah, with a cabinet and ministers. Cabinet ministers must be Afghan citizens and Moslems by faith. They are responsible to the legislative branch of

His Majesty Mohammed Zahir Shah

the government and remain in office until a prime minister resigns or is dismissed by the king, but individual members can be shifted at any time.

Afghanistan has a written constitution, but it is said that because of widespread illiteracy, many Afghans are not aware of it. Parts of the constitution are fashioned on those of European democracies as well as on the constitution of Iran, but the judicial branch of the government, which is most important, is based on the Sha'ri'at, Islamic law which governs almost every aspect of Moslem society, and which recognizes no regular code and does not distinguish between civil and criminal law.

The Sha'ri'at has to be interpreted, and is administered by theologians rather than by trained jurists. This makes for a clumsy and complicated system in which the courts are supposed to use both religious and secular laws in their application of justice. The Quazi, or judges, are appointed by the Minister of Justice, a post reserved for distinguished religious leaders, who in turn is expected to consult the Jamiyyat-i-Elema, a group of divines, on the religious angles of his work. However, the original power and influence of this group is on the wane, and it seems inevitable that the entire judicial structure of the country must eventually adapt itself to the pattern of a modern state.

His Majesty Mohammed Zahir Shah addressing Parliament

The Afghan parliament consists of the King, the House of Nobles, and the National Council. The House of Nobles sits throughout the year, and the National Council meets annually from May to October. The number of Nobles varies. The average is about twenty-five members, and they are appointed for life, whereas the representatives of the Council are elected by male suffrage for three-year terms, and number 171.

There is no party system in Afghanistan, and women do not have the vote. (Nor do they have it in Cambodia, Egypt, Iran, Iraq, Jordan, Laos, Libya, Liechtenstein, Nicaragua, Paraguay, Saudi Arabia, Switzerland, and Yemen.)

Elections are carried out under the provisions of the election law known as the Act of 1931, regarding elections to the National Council. Under this law suffrage is extended to Afghan subjects over twenty-one years of age, who must have at least one year's residence in their electoral district. The law excludes individuals under legal guardianship, bankrupt merchants, people with a criminal record, army personnel, and members of the municipal police.

Afghanistan is divided administratively into seven major and six minor provinces, and these in turn are divided into divisions, districts, and sub-districts or cantons. At the head of each major province there is a governor-general. The minor provinces are administered by a governor, the divisions by a commissioner, and the districts by a district-governor, or Hakim, of the locality. This system controls all but some of the tribal areas, and there is also an official in charge of nomad affairs, called a Hakim-i-Kuchi.

Public order in Afghanistan is maintained through the police and the gendarmerie. The police take care of the towns, and the gendarmerie maintain order throughout the rest of the country. It is generally agreed that this is an effective system, and a vast improvement on the past, when for centuries travelers in Afghanistan went in terror of their lives at the hands of bandits, and villages were forced to buy immunity by paying bribes to the robber gangs.

Amir Abd-er-Rahman Khan, ruler of Afghanistan from 1880 to 1901, is said to be responsible for the present effective system of police control, though his methods of bringing it about were rough indeed. As supreme ruler of the land he had it in his power to issue decrees and to see to it that they were enforced. On one occasion he was approached by an old man who handed him a petition, declaring that the police of the district were as bad as the bandits, that they persecuted the

Bicycles and gardis are popular
modes of transportation in Kabul today

people, carried off the women, stole property, and killed anyone who objected. Abd-er-Rahman Khan sent for the entire
contingent of police named by the old man, and had them
hanged there and then.

Both Abd-er-Rahman Khan and his son and successor,
Habibullah, were cruel and ruthless, but they did bring law
and order of a kind into a country which until then had known
little of either. Abd-er-Rahman Khan was a man of some wit.
It was he who observed—speaking of the rival ambitions of
Britain and Russia—"My country is like a poor goat on whom
the lion and the bear have both fixed their eyes!"

Two fifth-grade students locate Afghanistan on a papier-mâché globe

CHAPTER FOURTEEN

Education

Ideas have a way of creeping in where fools and even angels fear to tread, and it is hard to believe that Afghanistan can help but move forward in the direction of that first requirement for a modern state: a better education for all classes of the people, for the women as well as for the men.

So far, it has been estimated that ten per cent of the male population and less than ten per cent of the women are literate. There was a time when the education of young Afghans was in the hands of the Moslem clergy, the mullahs, and it consisted for the most part in learning passages from the Koran, which is the holy book of the Moslems, and in becoming familiar with the moral code and precepts of Islam.

The first secular school in Afghanistan was founded by King Habibullah. It is known as Habibiyeh (named after himself) and is situated in Kabul. Many of the leading men in Afghanistan today are graduates of this school, where, for the first time, the curriculum included not only religious instruction, but conventional subjects as taught in European schools. Habibullah employed Indian Moslems as teachers. He also founded a military school, staffed with a faculty of Turkish officers.

His son Amanullah founded three secondary schools, each of which taught a foreign language as its medium of instruction. Afghans have one great advantage in the matter of education: they are not plagued as are Indians and Ceylonese by a multiplicity of regional languages, which threatens to make a Tower of Babel in both those countries.

In Afghanistan, if Persian happens to be the predominant language of an area, it is taught there at the expense of Pashto, and vice versa. And it is interesting to note that this proud and suspicious people, who will not tolerate the activities of foreign religious missionaries, stress the teaching of foreign languages for their children. The Estaqlal School, for instance, has a French faculty, the Nejat School has English instructors, and today Americans are teaching at the Habibiyeh.

There are three levels of education—primary, secondary, and higher education. Primary education is free *and* compulsory. Almost any town of any size has its primary school, but these are poorly equipped, and such essential things as hardware, glass for windows, paper, pencils, ink, and so forth, are scarce and hard to obtain. Pupils generally are said to be alert and conscientious towards their work; they do not, as often happens in more fortunate countries, take their schooling for granted. In Afghanistan, as elsewhere in the East, people have an ingrained respect for scholarship, opportunity for study is regarded as a great privilege, and teachers are held in high respect.

For the young Afghan today, education may mean an entirely different way of life from that of his father and his grandfather. It may mean freedom from grueling poverty, emancipation from the dead hand of the past, a future in which for the first time the poor and underprivileged are given a chance to pick a career of their own choice.

The great problem in Afghan education is attendance. Parents expect their sons to work in the fields, where their labor is economically essential for the whole family. Many parents, uneducated themselves, fear that too much education will make their sons unhappy with simple village life, hard manual labor, and parental authority. And they look ahead to their own old age, to possible sickness or disablement, when, without sons to help out on the farm, life would become unbearable.

Altogether too many boys never do have a chance to complete the six years of primary education, and, despite the law which makes that education compulsory, they go home to help their fathers with the tilling of the fields, harvesting of crops, and shepherding of the flocks. One curious thing I noticed in Afghanistan was the look of maturity in the faces of quite young children. As in so many parts of the East, the period of carefree childhood seems very brief. By the time a boy is fourteen he has taken on many of the burdens of responsibility which, in more advanced societies, do not arrive until a man is twenty years old, or more.

Secondary education is also free, and some schools admit boarders whom the government supplies with uniforms and pocket money. Courses fall in two cycles of three years each. The first cycle emphasizes a general course of study; the second stresses mathematics, philosophy, and sociology. In the second cycle students may choose to take up English, German, or French.

They work in surroundings that would probably dishearten an American or an English child. The classrooms are generally bleak places without any kind of decoration to cheer them up, sometimes without paint on the walls or woodwork, and the equipment is poor, often inadequate, inaccurate, or obsolete.

As for the teachers, the best are those who have had the good luck to train abroad. Others suffer from inadequate training themselves, some with no more than a high-school education, and very few Afghan women teachers are likely to boast a diploma or other pedagogic requirement.

When I discussed this aspect of education with a young Afghan, he shrugged and said, "We are just beginning. Some-

Learning to read in a village school

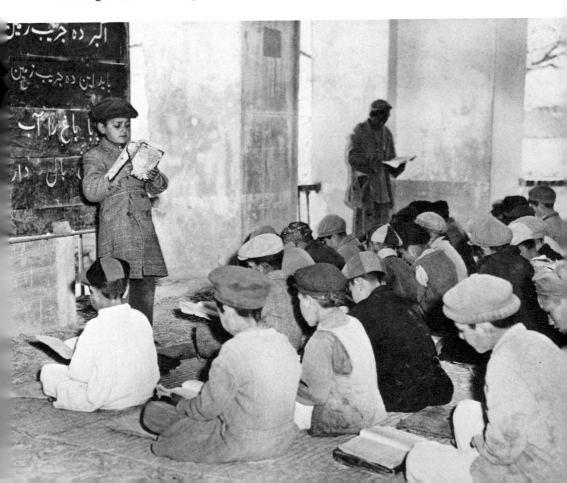

thing is better than nothing. It is better to have even a few books than paint on the walls. Better to *want* to learn, than to worry about the hardness of the bench, or the draft from a broken window. Better a teacher who is eager to share what he knows, than no teacher at all."

There is no doubt but that the greatest need in Afghanistan's educational system is for qualified teachers, and the government is pushing hard to expand its normal schools towards that end. The United States Agency of International Development has a contract with Teachers College, Columbia University, to help the Afghan Ministry of Education in teacher education as well as in the instruction of English.

The A.I.D. has also established an experimental high school, named Ibn Sina, where more than eight hundred boys are enrolled in the seventh, eighth and ninth classes. In addition, the A.I.D. has a contract with the University of Wyoming to provide instructors for the Vocational Agriculture School in Kabul, and another contract to provide a director and teachers for the Afghan Institute of Technology in Kabul.

Afghanistan has its university, the University of Kabul, called Puhantun, established in 1946, with an enrollment of about four hundred students. The university has faculties of Medicine, Science, Law, and Political Science, and all faculties offer four-year courses except the Faculty of Medicine, which requires six years.

The government gives free tuition to poorer students, as well as allowances for clothing and class supplies, and free board and lodging in Kabul. Half the faculty of the university are Afghans who received their doctorates from foreign universities. The rest mostly are German, French, Turkish, or Egyptian.

Most textbooks are in foreign languages, and the students

A class of third-graders shows eagerness to learn

deal with their subjects in French, English, or German. Here again the authorities have shown imagination and freedom from the petty national and regional rivalries which beset education in India and Ceylon. The new generation of Afghans are not made to suffer the confusion and frustration of having to struggle with two or three mediums of instruction, as is happening in Ceylon today, nor are they held up for months and years, waiting for the translation into Persian or Pashto of textbooks on subjects of such immediate importance, say, as medicine or physics.

Promising Afghan students are sent abroad to carry on their education in France, Germany, and the United States, and

Construction work on dormitory wing of University of Kabul

their expenses are paid by the Afghan government on condition that for each year of such foreign training the young man, on his return, must put in two years in government service.

The great flaw in the whole developing program of education in Afghanistan is the neglect of women's education. There are very few elementary or secondary schools for women in the whole country, and as of 1950, 31 of the University's 326 students and only nine of its 51 teachers were women. This is a shocking waste of vitality and intelligence, but perhaps not surprising when one considers that it stems from an ancient and ironbound tradition.

I find myself thinking of that attractive young headmistress of the girls' school at Kandahar, and her words to me at parting: "Someday things will be different. . . . They will be different even here, in Kandahar!"

CHAPTER FIFTEEN

Sports and Pastimes

If there is anything that will bring people of different cultures together, it is the love of sport. In addition to their own, Afghans have adopted a number of Western games such as soccer, hockey, basketball, and racing. Schoolboys usually select their favourite game and specialize in it, playing it throughout their school careers.

Each school has its particular team, and each team its distinctive uniform, as in America and elsewhere. Sporting events are looked forward to with great excitement and display of team spirit, as much by spectators as by players. In poor countries anything savoring of a spectacle is a welcome respite from the routine of everyday life, and people will come for miles, on foot, by bus, on donkey-back, to watch a game of wrestling or hockey or other matches of the kind.

Afghans take their sport very seriously and play strictly to win. They identify success or defeat with their own "side," or, when playing on an international level, with their country. Defeat is looked upon as humiliating in the extreme, and this makes for a hot contest even among the younger boys.

One of the Afghans' favorite sports is wrestling. Some schools are lucky enough to have gymnasiums, and in the larger cities or towns there are parks with space set apart to serve as an arena.

One form of wrestling is known as Gosai, and this is usually played before large crowds on festive occasions. Gosai may be played by as many men as want to take part, and the total is divided into two teams, usually of ten men apiece.

One Gosai player tries to make the goal by holding his right

Tribesmen beat drums in holiday celebration

leg behind his back with his left hand, and hopping on his left foot. The other members of his team run interference for him against the opposing team, and all the players move in the same fashion, hopping on one foot and holding the other behind their backs with their left hands. The game is played without pause from beginning to end, and is extremely strenuous. If the Gosai is knocked down before he makes the goal, his team loses, and the Gosai from the opposing team starts the next run. The winning team is the one which first succeeds in scoring the number of runs, or goals, which has been agreed on before the game begins.

The biggest spectacle and the most important game in Afghanistan is one known as Buz Kashi, or the Goat Game. This is held in as great popular esteem as cricket in England, or baseball in the United States, although it bears not the remotest kinship to either. If it resembles anything at all, it resembles polo, which also, incidentally, has its origins in the Middle East.

Buz Kashi has been called the sport of kings, and is said to have been brought to Afghanistan by Genghis Khan. And it certainly bears all the hallmarks of that bloodthirsty, violence-loving character, who is reported to have used the body of a defeated enemy instead of the present object or prize.

Buz Kashi is in a sense a variant of wrestling, except that it is played on horseback. The players are divided into teams, anywhere from ten to a thousand, the number depending on the region, the time of year, the degree of local wealth and so on.

To begin with a goat is killed and disemboweled, and the cavity filled with sand to give it weight. The carcass is placed in a shallow depression on the ground, a circle of white lime is drawn around the depression, and a post is placed at some distance on either side, making a sort of goal. The players, mounted on tough, high-spirited horses bred specially for the sport, collect beside the circle, and at a signal from the umpire they all converge on the carcass and fight for possession. What follows is a complete madhouse as one of the riders attempts to lift the carcass on to his saddle, while the opposing team tries to prevent his doing so and to get possession of the carcass themselves.

Once a rider has the carcass he gallops away with it at top speed, with his own team riding protection for him, and the rival team trying to break through and grab the prize. During the chase the riders stop at nothing to unseat the man carrying the carcass. There is neither fair play nor foul as they use hands, feet, and whips. Many of them, to keep their hands free, hold their whips between their teeth as they ride.

It is a fantastic and thrilling spectacle. Men are thrown and trampled, often seriously hurt, sometimes killed, but nothing stops the game as the carcass is snatched from one rider and passed to another. At times the entire field looks like a melee: struggling men, rearing, biting, snorting horses, curses, shouts, and flailing whips.

The rule is that the carcass has to be carried around one of the "goal" posts and then around the other, and the winner is he who manages to throw the prize, or what is left of it, into the circle of white lime, known as the Hallal.

Buz Kashi is played in the three northern provinces of Kataghan, Mazar-i-Sharif, and Maimana, but the present ruler of Afghanistan has elevated it to a national spectacle which demands only the most skilled and daring players and the hardiest and best trained mounts. Royal Buz Kashi is played on the king's birthday in October. This is a national holiday, and vast crowds converge on the capital and gather at the arena, a large plain where the game is played in the presence of the king, members of his household, and high officials of the realm.

Children in Kabul wear Pathan costumes for festival dances →

Buz Kashi is a brilliant spectacle, with crowds in holiday
attire, and rival teams, sometimes as many as three, consisting
of twenty men apiece, dressed in their respective uniforms.
One team will wear green and white, another maroon with
white karakul insignia on the back of the jacket, the third a
sort of reddish brown with high fawn-colored boots. All of
them wear fur-trimmed caps with pointed crowns, and every
man is mounted on a gaily caparisoned horse, tightly reined,
man and beast tense and ready for the fray.

Afghans enjoy numerous holidays, religious and secular. The
most important of the latter is No Ruz, which is Persian
in origin and which occurs on the first day of spring, March
21 or 22. This is a public holiday all over the country. Government and business offices close and country people stream

A bus stop in Charikar

into town wearing their best clothes, to marvel at the sights of the city, to flock to sporting events and carnivals, and to exchange calls with their friends.

Afghanistan has its Independence Day, celebrated on May 27, commemorating the breaking of all ties with Great Britain. At the end of August occurs Jashn-i-Isteqlal, a further celebration of independence, and this lasts for a week during which there are exhibitions of arts and crafts, military parades and reviews.

Religious holidays are taken very seriously throughout the country, and these follow the lunar calendar. Ramadan is the month of fasting when pious Moslems must abstain from food and drink from sunrise to sunset. The holiday of Id al-Fitre marks the end of this period, and is understandably one of great rejoicing, when people who can afford it eat and drink more than usual, to make up for the ordeal just past. Like all Moslems, Afghans observe their Sabbath on Friday, when everyone goes to the local mosque for prayers, and offices and business houses remain closed for the day.

Afghans seem to have a special gift for enjoying leisure, to which they give themselves whole-heartedly, playing cards, games of chess, engaging in sports and hunting, music and dancing, and endless conversations over the teacups and when smoking the traditional waterpipe. They love music and dancing, and many of the young men and boys learn how to play the drum or some stringed instrument, and think nothing of bursting into song whenever and wherever the mood takes them.

The national dance is called Atan, and is in great demand on national occasions. In the country it is danced by men, at night, round a fire. Other tribal dances are spirited and wild, the dancers working themselves into a frenzy, their black hair flying, eyes flashing, in the very spirit of abandon and love of rhythm.

Although gambling is generally regarded as contrary to the teaching of Islam, Afghans do occasionally bet on cockfights or a game of cards. Again, it is the women and girls who seem to lose out even in the area of relaxation, since their activities are restricted to conversation and cards, and most of their energies are taken up in preparing meals for family and guests.

Picnics might be described as Afghanistan's favorite national pastime, and whole families take off to the nearest park. Those who can afford a car or the price of a bus ticket go as far as the royal gardens at Paghman, sixteen miles outside Kabul.

I had come to Afghanistan by air from India, and I left it by air, flying from Kabul to Kandahar, thence to Teheran in

Iran. Once again I found myself in a DC-3, and this time the passengers numbered seven: four venerable Afghans on pilgrimage to Mohammed's birthplace in Mecca, a Canadian member of the World Health Organization, the Japanese ambassador to Kabul, and myself. The remaining seats had been removed to make room for bales of karakul skins being shipped for sale in Teheran.

Westward we flew, a tiny speck in an endless sky above endless miles of bleached desert, mountain peaks, dry ravines and microscopic dots of green where a sparse moisture had been caught in some declivity, and held.

I looked at the four old Afghan gentlemen in their seats across

An impromptu outdoor concert in the King's gardens at Paghman

the aisle. Three had their eyes closed and were murmuring prayers, the amber-beaded rosaries held in their gnarled fingers. The fourth was gazing out of his window, and once, when he turned his turbanned head, I caught an expression of awe and wonder in his eyes. No doubt his own parents had made the haj, or pilgrimage to Mecca, by foot and donkey-back, or by ocean from the shores of what is now Pakistan, and it must have taken months, perhaps years, to complete the journey to Arabia and back. Now, this old man and his companions would make it by air in a matter of days.

Looking out of my own window I could see, eight or nine thousand feet below, a cluster of infinitesimal black specks beside a larger speck of miraculous green. A nomad encampment beside an oasis, hundreds of miles from the nearest road, the nearest town, pausing in their immemorial travels, perhaps to glance upward at the glittering wings of our plane, perhaps to marvel at our adventure as I could not help but marvel at theirs.

Glossary

Ababil   a robin-sized bird with forked tail and iridescent plumage.

Afghani   the Afghan monetary unit; about twenty afghanis equal one American dollar.

Aina Massaf   one form of the Afghan marriage ceremony, meaning the meeting in the mirror: bride and groom hold a mirror and see each other for the first time in this way.

Aqa   Persian for Mr.

Atan   the national dance of Afghanistan.

Badal   a part of the Pathan code of honor: the obligation to wipe out dishonor by the shedding of blood. Vendetta.

Buz Kashi   the most spectacular and most popular Afghan sport: the goat game, a variant of wrestling played on horseback.

Chadri   a billowy garment which covers the wearer from head to toe and which is compulsory dress for Afghan women in public.

Chai khana   an Afghan village teahouse which serves as a social center for rest, refreshment, and exchange of news.

Chapan   a long buttonless coat worn by men in northern Afghanistan.

Charpoy   a string bedstead.

Dasht   a desert, such as the Dasht-i-Margo.

Dushizeh   Persian for Miss.

Gardi   a two-wheeled carriage.

Gosai   a popular Afghan sport.

Guru   a teacher in India, especially a religious teacher.

Haj   the traditional pilgrimage to Mecca, birthplace of the Prophet Mohammed, which is the sacred duty of every Moslem.

Hakim   a district-governor of a locality in Afghanistan.

155

Hakim-i-kuchi   an Afghan government official in charge of nomad affairs.

Hallal   a circle of white lime into which Buz Kashi players must throw goat carcass.

Id al-Fitre   a religious holiday of great rejoicing which marks the end of the month of fasting for Moslems.

Jamiyyat-i-Elema   an important group of Moslem theologians in Afghanistan.

Jashn-i-Isteqlal   the annual independence day celebration in Afghanistan which occurs at the end of August.

Jihad   Moslem holy war.

Jirga   a dignified council of elders which serves as a kind of parliament to settle domestic disputes among tribes of the North-West Frontier.

Karez   an ingenious method of irrigation whereby water from permanent water tables is channeled underground to agricultural areas of Afghanistan.

Kebab   a skewer of broiled mutton, typical Afghan food.

Khaki   an English word derived from clothing worn by Khattaks, famous tribe of the North-West Frontier.

Khan   literally, a lord or prince; a kind of honorific, similar to the English "Sir," which indicates social position and prestige.

Khel   a tribe.

Kuchis   Afghan nomads.

Malik   a tribal chief of the Pathans.

Mast   yoghurt, popular among Afghan nomads.

Merman   Pashto for Mrs.

Milmastia   a part of the Pathan code of honor: the obligation to proffer open-handed hospitality.

Mullah   a member of the Islamic theocratic order who wield great power and influence in Afghanistan.

Naan   typical Afghan bread, made of whole wheat which is pressed into flat cakes and then baked in an oven.

Nanawatai   a part of the Pathan code of honor: the obligation to grant asylum to the fugitive.

No Ruz   the most important Afghan secular holiday, Persian in origin and celebrated on the first day of spring.

Pakhtunali   the code of honor of the Pathan tribesmen of the North-West Frontier.

Perleh   Pashto for Miss.

Postin   a goatskin jacket worn by Afghan nomads with the fur next to the body, sometimes decorated with embroidery.

Puls   small nickel or copper coins; there are 100 puls in one afghani.

Quazi   judges of Afghanistan, appointed by the Minister of Justice on the advice of theologians.

Ramadan   the month of fasting during which pious Moslems abstain from food from sunrise to sunset.

Roghan   mutton fat used for cooking.

Shagali   Pashto for Mr.

Sha'ri'at   Islamic law which governs almost every aspect of Moslem society.

Shuma   formal second person, used for everyone.

Tandur   a typical Afghan oven: a circular, clay-lined pit with a charcoal fire at the bottom.

Tu   informal second person, used for children, lower-class people, and close friends.

Yurt   a tent of the nomadic tribes in northern Afghanistan, roughly dome-shaped with a wooden frame covered by pieces of felt.

Index

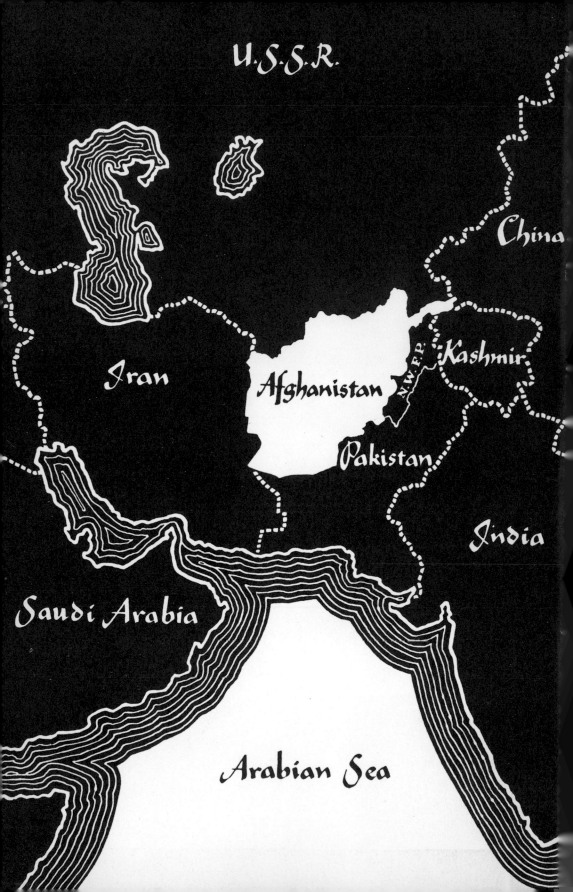